General Editor Alastair Service

THE BUILDINGS OF BRITAIN
STUART AND BAROQUE

D1166114

Richard Morrice holds a PhD from the University of Reading, where he took a BA in History of Art and Architecture, studying under Professor Kerry Downes. He is a Member of the Architectural Committee of the Bath Preservation Trust.

Alastair Service is the author of *Edwardian Architecture* (1977), *The Architects of London: 1066 to the present day* (1979), *A Guide to the Megaliths of Europe* (1979, paperback 1981), *Edwardian Interiors* (1982) and other books. He is a Committee Member of the Victorian Society.

Uniform with this volume in the series *The Buildings of Britain*:

ANGLO-SAXON AND NORMAN
Alastair Service

TUDOR AND JACOBEAN
Malcolm Airs

REGENCY
David Watkin

Titles in preparation:
MEDIEVAL AND GOTHIC
GEORGIAN
VICTORIAN
TWENTIETH CENTURY

General Editor Alastair Service

THE BUILDINGS OF BRITAIN
STUART AND BAROQUE

A Guide and Gazetteer
RICHARD MORRICE

Barrie & Jenkins

London Melbourne Sydney Auckland Johannesburg

For my parents

Barrie & Jenkins Ltd
An imprint of the Hutchinson Publishing Group
17–21 Conway Street, London W1P 6JD

Hutchinson Group (Australia) Pty Ltd
30–32 Cremorne Street, Richmond South, Victoria 3121
PO Box 151, Broadway, New South Wales 2007

Hutchinson Group (NZ) Ltd
32–34 View Road, PO Box 40–086, Glenfield, Auckland 10

Hutchinson Group (SA) (Pty) Ltd
PO Box 337, Bergvlei 2012, South Africa

Designed and produced for Barrie & Jenkins Ltd by
Bellew & Higton Publishers Ltd
17–21 Conway Street, London WIP 6JD

First published 1982

© Richard Morrice 1982

For illustration copyrights, see Illustration Acknowledgements

Photoset in Goudy Old Style
by V & M Graphics Ltd, Aylesbury, Bucks
Printed and bound in Great Britain by
Penshurst Press Ltd

ISBN 0 09 150430 9 (cased)
ISBN 0 09 150431 7 (paper)

CONTENTS

ACKNOWLEDGEMENTS

Having thought about seventeenth- and early eighteenth-century architecture for some years I have been influenced by too many people, through reading and conversation, to acknowledge them all by name. My thanks are, however, due to several who have given specific encouragement, help and advice. Kerry Downes, who first awoke my interest in the subject, has helped in many ways, especially in supplying illustrations, reading the manuscript, suggesting alterations and answering queries on Wren. Pete Smith also read, advised, listened and gave me the benefit of his knowledge of the baroque country house. Nigel Silcox-Crowe answered questions about Sir Roger Pratt and architecture during the Commonwealth. In addition thanks are due to Jane Hoos, Robin Inshaw and Richard Holder for less specific help and encouragement. Finally, I must thank Mary for criticism, patience and support.

PREFACE

History does not divide easily into self-sufficient periods, each with a beginning and an end, and this is especially true of architecture. Thus, while the core of this study is the period from the beginning of the Civil War in 1642 to the death of Queen Anne in 1714, consideration is also given to earlier developments and the late lag after 1714. The great innovator of Stuart architecture, Inigo Jones, was an Elizabethan by birth and built most of his important works in a period dominated by Jacobean styles. Similarly, baroque buildings continued to appear well into Georgian times, when Palladianism was leading advanced architectural taste. Thus adequately to cover the Stuart styles of Pratt and May, the influence of Wren and the baroque of Hawksmoor, Vanbrugh and Archer, mention is also made of the proto-Palladianism of Jones and Webb, as well as the use of the baroque after 1714 by Hawksmoor, Vanbrugh and provincial architects.

This book gives an account of the building-types that architects of the seventeenth and early eighteenth centuries were most accustomed to build. I have considered it important to explain in an introductory chapter two developments that such a treatment might overlook – the evolution of the styles of the period, and that of the actual practice of architecture and the way that architects went about their business. The seventeenth century was a period of crisis throughout Europe, and one not only of much turbulence in political and religious life in Britain but also of great vitality in the sciences and arts. This was reflected in the considerable changes in the practice of architecture at this time, most notably in the switch from a late medieval system of building to one that more nearly approximates to the organisation of the architectural profession during the nineteenth century, if not to the institutionalised system of the present day. It must be stressed again, however, that this was a period of transition, and as at all such times variety of practice was the overriding fact; this has in the past clouded the issue and provoked misleading accounts of the architectural history of the time.

Within the typological framework of this book, concentration on both regional trends and on the careers of individual architects has tended to become submerged. Stress is laid, however, on the importance of certain architects, such as Jones, Pratt, Wren, Hawksmoor and Vanbrugh, who all made vigorous personal contributions to the architectural history of the period. Wales is treated very much as an architectural province of England, while Scotland tends to be dealt with separately, having a definite architectural development and flavour of its own.

The structure of this book follows the five main types of building. Country houses were the forcing ground of architectural development during the period and thus figure most prominently, divided between two chapters. The first of these considers the contribution of Inigo Jones and the development of the post-Restoration house, a timeless British building-type that continued to be of importance throughout the eighteenth century, as well as the Scottish move away from the medieval tower-house tradition into styles more European in scope. The second discusses the influence of European baroque styles on interior decoration and on external architecture, with reference both to palace and country house building, and emphasises the growth of regional baroque schools. Town houses and vernacular buildings in the country are considered much less fully and it has been possible in the space available only to touch on the huge variety of buildings from which all country areas and most towns derive a great degree of their character.

The history of the church during this period was dominated by the figure of Wren, who not only designed the greatest cathedral to be built, or even begun, in this country since the Reformation but also realised that Anglican liturgy could not be adequately practised in the churches left by the Reformation and therefore established a form more suitable for it, one that was to survive well into the later eighteenth century. By contrast, in the history of British church-building the New Churches Commission of 1711, with its small number of magnificent churches by Hawksmoor, Archer and others, is something of a footnote with little influence, but in the broad perspective of the history of architecture in England provided the last great concentration of English baroque buildings. Buildings of benevolence were also characteristic of the age that followed the Reformation in that until that time the roles of caring for the sick and elderly and education had been taken largely by the church. The numbers of schools, hospitals and almshouses that survive from this period, from the grandest to the most humble, serve as reminders that the carrying out of these functions, though haphazard, had a continuous history.

The subject of the short final chapter, public buildings, is the most enigmatic, as few were built during this period, and those which survive are mostly small-scale and modest. The exceptions to this rule were the work of the Board of Ordnance, which remains shrouded in mystery in that an extremely Vanbrughian collection of buildings seems to have had little or no connection with him, and the commercial buildings of the City of London have nearly all been demolished or remodelled. Public building was of less importance at this time than later.

1

INTRODUCTION:
THEORY AND PRACTICE

Uppark, West
Sussex, c. 1690, by
William Talman.
Post-Restoration
Stuart house
typical of many
throughout the
country: centre of
garden façade

At the beginning of the seventeenth century architectural tradition in Britain was still basically medieval. Certainly there was an overlay of Renaissance motifs and ideas, but they were applied to a tradition that stretched back far into the past. Windows, often in shallow, many-lighted bays, were large, chimneys tall and elaborate, and Gothic details, such as window tracery, not unknown. Houses were long, low and tended to sprawl, retaining the late medieval plan of central great hall with great chamber above. In Scotland houses were even more traditional, the tower-house remaining popular until the later seventeenth century. The Jacobean timber-framed house, with its complexity of decoration, plan and silhouette, lingered on in some parts of England until the 1680s, while churches continued to be built in the perpendicular style, though often simplified, using the medieval plan of chancel, nave and aisles. By the Restoration this tradition had been largely replaced by Classicism, one of the consequences of the general European interest in antique civilisation, that had grown increasingly important in Britain during the sixteenth century.

Classicism in architecture is not just a type of decoration but a system in which all parts of a building are locked into each other proportionally, producing harmony between the parts. Amongst Tudor and Jacobean builders there had been only the most sketchy idea of how this proportioning worked and on the whole their buildings remained pragmatic solutions to the problems of building grand houses in the tradition of medieval architecture. Although the columns and pilasters, and the entablatures – the uprights and crossbeams – of the Classical orders – Tuscan, Doric, Ionic, etc. – were known, they were regarded merely as part of the Italian style of decoration by Elizabethan and Jacobean architects and were used accordingly. From the time of the building of the royal palaces for Henry VIII until well into the seventeenth century there were few Englishmen who regarded Classicism as anything more than a source of decorative motifs. This attitude was only superseded by the advent of an architect who truly understood the underlying principles of Classical architecture and its use of the order: Inigo Jones.

From 1605 Jones enjoyed Court patronage as a designer of Masques, the spectacular theatrical entertainments fashionable at Court at this time; from 1615, after his second trip to Italy, as Surveyor of the King's Works he gave to architecture the same combination of artistic sense and intellect that characterised the artists and architects of the Italian Renaissance. Jones's buildings have the simplicity, calmness and legibility typical of the architecture of the High Renaissance in Italy in the years between 1500 and 1520. He

Palazzo Caprini, Rome, known as the House of Raphael, 1513; Donato Bramante. The definitive High Renaissance Roman Palace in the simplest of Classical styles

Raph Vrbinat ex Lapide Coctili Romæ, ex structum

showed no willingness, certainly on the exteriors of his buildings, to indulge either in the fantasy that was so popular in England during the later years of the sixteenth century, or in the more sophisticated experiments that were developing in the baroque in Rome at the very time that he was building.

Jones was prompted to turn towards a purer Classicism by his second visit to Italy between 1613 and 1615, when he travelled with the Earl of Arundel to the Veneto, the mainland area around Venice, met the aged Vincenzo Scamozzi and picked up a large number of Palladio's and his pupil Scamozzi's architectural drawings and designs. Andrea Palladio, the architect who had led a Classical revival in the Veneto during the third quarter of the sixteenth century and had been Scamozzi's tutor, was the chief reason for Jones's visit; he annotated his copy of Palladio's *Four Books of Architecture* (first published in Venice in 1570) when studying the buildings and thereby instituted a tradition of homage to Palladio that was to remain standard for British architects until well into this century. Palladio's book offered many simple, plain solutions to the contemporary problems of public and private building in a Classical style more authentically based on the antique than that of earlier Italian architects. His fame was sealed by the publication of these designs in simple form, part architectural manual, part pattern book. It is to Jones's credit that, though influenced by the simplicity and appeal of the antique in Palladio's buildings, he was no mere copyist and his buildings are more than mere variations of Palladian prototypes.

Sir John Summerson was the first to notice that, far from petering out when Jones began to build, Jacobean architecture subtly changed to become a style that combined elements from Jacobean and Jonesian as well as Flemish and Dutch seventeenth-century architecture. He named this rather amorphous style 'artisan mannerism'. Precise definition is meaningless because, the style being based on such a wide variety of sources, there was little stylistic consensus among the masons and builders who used it from around 1630 almost to the end of the century. Further modification stemmed from a new generation of architectural pattern books imported into Britain. Although this influence can be overestimated it is undoubtedly true that, while Jacobean architecture had taken its ornament from compilations of decoration, artisan mannerism seems to have drawn inspiration rather from books which illustrated buildings. The growth in importance of the compact house type, the single block, although stemming from Jones ultimately, in most cases of its use between 1630 and 1670 was almost as much influenced by Rubens's *Palazzi di Genova* (1622), which showed a large number of single-block houses with roofs and tall chimneys. Although definition is not easy, artisan mannerist buildings are easily recognisable, not only for the common use of Dutch-type curving gables, but also for their frequent use of high-quality brickwork and of features that were out-of-date compared with contemporary London practice. Thus an early example like Swakeleys, a house of 1630 in north-west

Palazzo Balbi-Senarega, Genoa, c. 1610–1618; Bartolomeo Bianco. A typically tall Genoese palace as illustrated in Rubens's *Palazzi di Genova*

III.   Facciata del Palazzo de gli sig.ri Giacomo e Pantaleo Balbi.

Swakeleys,
London Borough
of Hillingdon,
1630. Typical
artisan mannerist
blend of Jacobean
and Flemish motifs
in a symmetrical
scheme

London, has such obsolete features as prominent bow-windows (without the simple cross form of single transom and mullion that Jones had used at the Queen's House and elsewhere), together with windows of differing size and with no regularity in the fenestration across the façade, except in so far as the window disposition is symmetrical. Similarly the house's interior is organised in the tradition of Jacobean houses. Later in the century a modification of artisan mannerism appeared, exemplified by Sudbury Hall in Derbyshire of the 1660s and 1670s, which, while acknowledging the innovations of such houses as Sir Roger Pratt's Coleshill House in Oxfordshire, still used overlarge windows with tracery, a two-storey frontispiece, itself a Jacobean motif, with decoration in the same tradition, diapered brickwork and a very late example of the long gallery. Late examples of artisan mannerism continued to appear even into the eighteenth century, mostly in buildings of a vernacular nature such as

farmhouses and cottages, and especially almshouses.

An Anglo-Flemish style of sorts was also apparent in Scotland, introduced possibly by William Wallace, in which the tradition of the Scottish fortified house known as the tower-house, in its later manifestation (1560–1640), was allied with the quadrangular (rather than L or Z) plan and with decoration that derived from English and Flemish styles, best seen at Heriot's Hospital in Edinburgh or Drumlanrig Castle in Dumfries and Galloway. Wallace was no Jones, however, and Scotland had to wait until Bruce for an architect with a comparable understanding of Classicism. In less prestigious buildings such as provincial country churches one finds medieval traditions, perhaps with half-understood Classical decoration, clinging on well into the eighteenth century.

The later modification of artisan mannerism, influenced less by Jacobean traditions and Dutch architecture and more by Jones, Pratt and Italy, exemplified by Balls Park, Hertfordshire, Thorpe Hall, Cambridgeshire and Sudbury Hall, had its high-point during the Civil War and Commonwealth, a time of reduced building activity for the nobility and, of course, the Court, but of greater freedom for those members of the gentry who supported Parliament and who continued building to a modest extent. The Civil War and Commonwealth, because of their interruption of architectural practice, gave architects the opportunity to travel and this indicated their interests, showing the way that architecture would develop after the Restoration. Pratt visited the Veneto and France, while Hugh May studied Dutch red-brick Classicism and the baroque interior decoration of the royal palaces of France. John Webb remained at home and continued the Palladian tradition begun by Jones.

Classicism with its precise rules of operation was taken up with enthusiasm in Britain because it reflected the very seventeenth-century idea that reason was the basis for the ordering and functioning of the universe and everything therein. It is, therefore, not surprising that Wren, one of the leading scientists of the generation that saw the foundation of the Royal Society to gather and codify knowledge, should become interested in architecture, because he recognised that the experimentation which he applied to natural phenomena could also be applied to the design of buildings. This scientific attitude led to the great variety of churches he designed for the City of London after the Great Fire, literally a series of experiments in Anglican church design – as Kerry Downes has

Sudbury Hall, Derbyshire, c. 1660–80. Decoration of porch by Sir William Wilson; the balustrade was moved from the roof-top in the nineteenth century

expressed it, the architecture of trial and error. A similar empirical approach, that is one based on observation and experiment rather than theory, can be seen in the history of the early projects for St Paul's, where Wren refused to allow himself to be tied down on the final appearance of the Cathedral. As the Wren style was based more on observation than theory it was more susceptible to the practical demands of country builders, which explains the high standard of provincial building after the Restoration compared to the relative crudity of earlier attempts to copy Jones's highly intellectual Italianate Classicism.

This scientific attitude to architecture is one explanation for the restricted acceptance of the baroque in Britain. As a stylistic term baroque refers to the art and architecture of Europe during the 150 years after 1600. In architecture it is typified by the style of Rome during the forty years around 1650, the principal features of which have been identified by Anthony Blunt: 'a preference for a large scale, the use of irregular and complex forms, movement in line, mass and space, a fusion of the arts of painting and sculpture with architecture, the bold use of illusionism and directed light, dramatic action extended over architectural space, and richness of materials'. The problem with the concept of an English baroque style, however, is not whether any of the properties listed above are applicable to English architecture but that the baroque was heavily identified during the seventeenth century with ideas antithetical to English sensibilities, often violently so. The baroque in Europe served, firstly, Catholicism in its spiritual and temporal expansion after the set-backs of the Reformation, and was thus to the English a source of some anxiety. Secondly, the baroque was the Court art of Louis XIV and therefore of an expansionist absolute monarchy regarded as a threat in England not only to the nascent constitutional monarchy but also, because of France's territorial ambitions, to English economic and political ambitions. As a non-Catholic, non-absolutist country, England must not be too lightly identified with the baroque; at the same time, architecture that, given the above definitions, can only be described as baroque is clearly to be seen in this country beginning with the south front of Chatsworth, Derbyshire (1687–89).

In the hands of Hawksmoor and Vanbrugh after 1700 the English baroque is often seen as having taken a strange and independent turn, but in fact it relied on much the same motivations and interests as the baroque of other countries. Interest in the architecture of the past, and in all periods inclusively, was the foundation for the eclecticism of these architects and not only Wren, Hawksmoor, Vanbrugh, Archer and Talman, but also Fischer von Erlach in Vienna, Schlüter in Berlin and Juvarra in Turin, and underlay the formlessness of the careers of each, which lacked a perceptible development and structure by which their buildings can be understood. The emotional and intellectual drive of the English baroque led not to the revival of the architecture of antiquity (or of any other time) but to the romantic expression of the idea of Classical building, with all its overtones of learning, magnificence and, above all, the heroism of Classical times. As Kerry Downes has put it, the strangeness of many English baroque buildings, particularly those by Hawksmoor, can be explained only as the 'evocativeness of unnameable memories', the product of the complex blending of memory and imagination.

It was inevitable that this most extreme of styles should eventually be overtaken by one less emotional and personal. Palladianism was a more easily copied style than the baroque of Hawksmoor or Vanbrugh because it relied on the publication of two books in which could be found not only the architectural ideals of the movement but also patterns to be followed in the designing of buildings. The first intimations of a change in thinking appeared in 1712, the date of the writing of the Earl of Shaftesbury's *Letter concerning Design*, an early and vigorous anti-baroque polemic which did not, however, circulate widely until much later. The first book to be generally available was *Vitruvius Britannicus* by Colen Campbell. Though it illustrated most of the major baroque houses in the country, the text specifically attacked the baroque, though of the continental variety, and exhorted patrons and architects to turn to the examples of Palladio and Jones. Palladio was also celebrated in the publication of the first English translation of his *Four Books on Architecture*, published in 1716. Although the publication of *Vitruvius Britannicus* in three parts between 1715 and 1725 was Campbell's most polemical contribution to the debate, he had earlier built a house demonstrating his ideas at Wanstead in Essex (c. 1713). As John Harris has said, there is nothing in English architecture quite like the unadorned block of Wanstead House, which must have come as a considerable shock after such baroque masterpieces as Castle Howard, Blenheim and Heythrop.

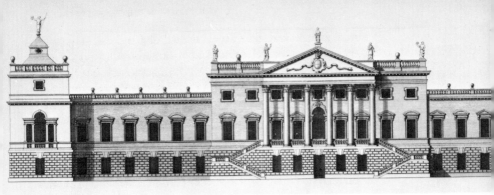

There is no consensus as to the date that English baroque ended and Palladianism started; the baroque did not suddenly stop and Palladianism take over. The transition must lie somewhere between the date of Shaftesbury's essay and the final victory of the Palladian school in the complete takeover of the Office of Works sometime in the 1730s. Baroque did not even then completely die out and can still be seen in attitudes to detail and interior decoration well after 1750, no doubt to some extent influenced by the continuing European Late Baroque. Leoni and Gibbs, however, trimmed their baroque personal styles because they realised that in order to get commissions lip-service would have to be paid to the prevailing fashion.

In its veneration of Jones, Palladianism was the full circle turned for English architecture. With Palladianism, and the replacement of the country mason-builder by the more learned provincial architect, came a greater uniformity of architectural style and standard throughout the country. The story of the victory of Palladianism, important though it may be to explain the decline of the baroque, belongs, however, to a later volume; worthy of respect, though, was Campbell's perception that battles of taste were won only in the field of country house building.

Jones's novel infusion of the tradition of building with a new artistic sense as well as the rigorous intellectual discipline of Italianate Classicism led to a completely new status for the architect. Jones was not a practical builder, mason or workman in the Elizabethan sense but a courtier. He regarded himself more as the equal of nobility and seems to have been accepted as such by members of that class; certainly, whereas previously the mason would have bowed to the wishes of his

Wanstead House, Essex, third design, 1720; Colen Campbell. As built except for the end-pavilions

patron in all features of the artistic design of a building, Jones was allowed a more or less free hand in both the artistic and technical aspects of the building, and may thus be termed the first true architect in Britain. This rise in the status of architecture was important also because it allowed educated people to become architects where previously they would have considered designing buildings only for themselves. However, it is important to stress that there were many ways in which buildings could be built during the seventeenth and early eighteenth centuries. For instance, houses exist from this period that came into being in all the following ways: an architect designed the building and supervised the work; architect designed and mason built; mason designed and built; patron designed and mason built; and various other combinations of these. At the end of the period Lord Burlington was as much a professional architect as many of his contemporaries who were not in his happy position of having the wherewithal to indulge his interests; but then few indeed were the architects before 1750 who had actually been trained as such.

The question of authorship of a building becomes even more complex when it is realised that the master-plasterer and brick-layer, the joiner and carpenter, had almost complete control over the work for which they were engaged and would even hire their own labourers. Therefore, as H. M. Colvin has shown, in the example of a house begun at Hampstead Marshall, Berkshire, c. 1663, the master-craftsmen submitted designs for the decorative features which the architect then signed, showing that he approved. Similarly, though the staircase would be given in a rough form on the plans by the architect, the ornamentation of it was normally left to the imagination of the craftsman who built it.

The importance of master-craftsmen was reflected in their presence in various posts in the Office of Works. This organisation, and its counterpart the Scottish Royal Works, had responsibility for all royal buildings, and acted as a centre around which the most important architects gathered; its employment of craftsmen and masons, along with the boom in London building after the Fire, allowed London styles and standards to percolate through to the provinces. At any one time a broad similarity of style is perceptible in the buildings commissioned from the Office. It is not surprising that during the later period of Wren's Surveyorship the house style was the baroque or that Lord Burlington, who wished to replace baroque with Palladianism, should have made such an effort to win the Office for his own men. The situation in Scotland was broadly similar, though the practice was to appoint an administrator to the post of Master of Work, and to engage an architect as the Master-mason to the Scottish Crown. Two of the most considerable architects did, however, become Master – Sir William Bruce and James Smith – and the more important buildings of the time show the influence of the Works style, in a manner similar to that of non-royal buildings in England.

The foregoing is a short sketch of the conditions which shaped architectural practice during the seventeenth and early eighteenth centuries. It was an immensely complex period, corresponding in architectural terms to the early modern period of historical study, and represents the dividing line between medieval architecture with its craft-oriented, overwhelmingly vernacular pattern and the professionalism and internationalism of modern times. Unfortunately our detailed knowledge of much of the background in which the buildings must be set and from which they sprang is incomplete, although a fuller picture is emerging. Recent research, in particular, has uncovered a great deal that has altered our perception of how country houses developed and the way in which they were used. As the most important formal building type in terms of architectural development the country house will be discussed first.

2

THE STUART
COUNTRY HOUSE

Country house building during the first sixty years of the seventeenth century was dominated by the gradual development of a Classical type of house. Inigo Jones, more than any other man responsible for bringing an understanding of Classicism to England, did not build any country houses, though he did design two buildings for the Crown that were to be of great importance for the course of English architecture in general, and country house building in particular. The first, the Queen's House in Greenwich, was really a villa (the Italian term for a country house not far from town). It was begun in 1616 for Anne of Denmark, James I's Queen, though it was not completed until 1635 for her successor, Henrietta Maria, after being redesigned about 1630. It would have been a small building of great simplicity were it not for the strange plan Jones was forced to give it because the gardens of Greenwich Palace, as then organised, were divided from the park by the Woolwich road. Thus Jones built the house with a block on either side of the road connected by a central spinal bridge, giving the house an H-shaped plan, so that the Queen could pass between the two parts of the palace without crossing the road. (In 1661 bridges were added either side of this spine which made the block appear more cube-like). Otherwise the Queen's House is completely straightforward with a strikingly unadorned river-front and a first-floor loggia on the other side, facing south and taking advantage of the sun. The decoration of the interior was never completed, the only room worthy of note being the two-storey hall with its wooden gallery.

The Queen's House was finished over a decade after the completion of Jones's most elaborate building, the Banqueting

House in Whitehall (1619–22), intended as a permanent home for the entertainments the Crown customarily gave. The main front, actually the side of the building, shows very well just how capable Jones was in handling the Classical repertory. Two storeys articulated by a superimposed order break forward in the middle three bays to give a central emphasis and thus balance to the composition. The outer bays are articulated by pilasters, the central ones by half-columns, increasing that emphasis. It is a virtuoso performance of balanced, simple, legible Classicism, showing perfectly Jones's understanding of the style as one of more than mere decoration. The interior is spatially simple because its use for entertainment required a large open hall which could be decorated easily as occasion demanded. The large double-cube surrounded by a gallery supported on Ionic columns is completed by a ceiling of novel design. Although plasterwork of the Jacobean type was becoming simpler at the time, with panels of larger size being surrounded by thicker borders, the whole Banqueting House ceiling consists of only nine panels, the central one oval and the rest rectangular, separated by extremely ornate and deep borders. The decoration of these borders is based on the Classical repertory of acanthus leaves, volute-scrolls and so forth, developed from Italian experiments in antique decoration via France.

Queen's House, Greenwich, 1616–19, completed 1630–35; Inigo Jones. The Classical simplicity of the south façade is enlivened by loggia

Above: Banqueting House, Whitehall, London, 1619–22; Inigo Jones. An Italian High Renaissance palace façade with central emphasis

Right: The main room, a double cube with compartmented ceiling framing paintings by Rubens

Of all the contemporary country houses in which Jones may have been involved the most likely is Raynham Hall in Norfolk, built during the 1620s and 1630s for Sir Roger Townshend by William Edge. It combines two novel features, possibly drawn from Jones's Prince's Lodging at Newmarket (1619), a central great hall (still with the screens passage of Jacobean houses) and the temple portico. The great hall of the

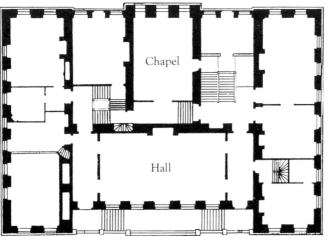

Above: Raynham Hall, Norfolk, begun 1621. Garden façade with portico to great chamber

Left: Plan of Raynham Hall. Jacobean great hall with a pair of screens passages fitted symmetrically into the Classical house plan

Chapel

Hall

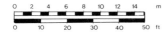

Prince's Lodging had probably been placed in the centre of the ground floor of the entrance-front, and this was the position chosen for Raynham, with the added distinction that the status of the high great chamber above was indicated on the exterior of the building by the garden-front portico. Townshend succeeded, therefore, in moulding the Jacobean house-plan into a suitable shape for the Jonesian symmetrical exterior, a compromise that was resolved only some thirty years later.

Contrary to tradition Jones does not seem to have been involved in the building of Wilton House near Salisbury. Wilton, for the Earl of Pembroke, seems to have been designed by Isaac de Caus who was at this time (1636) collaborating with Jones on the Bedford Estate in Covent Garden. As originally conceived the house was to have been almost twice as long as the surviving south front, with a pitched roof and the great room of state (the high great chamber) on the first floor behind a hexastyle portico, a plan similar to Raynham. The house was gutted by fire in about 1648 and it was rebuilt by John Webb, Jones's pupil and main follower, who added the towers and refitted the interiors, including the single-cube and double-cube suite of the south front, with which there is no evidence that Jones was involved. The scheme definitely followed Jones's ideas, which though stipulating reticence on the exterior of a building did, however, allow for great show and splendour inside.

Wilton House, Wiltshire, 1636; Isaac de Caus. Rebuilt after 1648; John Webb. The towers added by Webb became a stock Palladian motif

Webb was the only architect to follow Jones's example and his houses were probably the only ones to be built, apart from those above, which give any real indication of Jones's intentions vis-à-vis the smaller country house. Webb has rightly been considered the first professionally trained architect in England, assisting Jones as he did for many years, and he was one of the very few architects, rather than masons or builders, who remained active in the country during the Commonwealth, rather than taking the advantage of the lack of patronage to travel abroad. His earliest work, at Lamport Hall in Northamptonshire (1655–57), was the building of a single wing, the central five bays projecting and rusticated, with greater emphasis given by a pediment raised up and behind the parapet balustrade. At The Vyne, Hampshire (1654–56), a further ill-conceived Jonesianism was added to the Elizabethan house in the form of the first free-standing portico to be built in England, added to the garden-front, while the fenestration was tidied up to make it look more symmetrical. More successful was Gunnersbury Park outside London (1658–63; now destroyed), an extremely plain house very much in Jones's tradition with a pedimented portico on the entrance-front. Amesbury Abbey, Wiltshire (c. 1661), another Jones-Palladio villa, is the most successful of Webb's houses, with a shallow ground-storey and higher first-floor, both rusticated, and with prominent key-stones over the windows. This porticoed house proved a potent source of inspiration for architects of the Palladian-Jonesian revival during the next century.

Interesting though these houses of Webb's undoubtedly are, they exerted little influence on the country house after the Restoration. Much more important was a slightly earlier house, Coleshill in Oxfordshire, begun c. 1650 by Sir Roger Pratt for his cousin, and the prototype for a tradition of country-house design that was to last almost a century (the house is sadly now demolished). Pratt's revolution was to remove the last vestige of medieval usage from the hall, its function as the place where the servants ate; he provided a separate servants' hall in the basement. The hall was now vacant and so Pratt placed the main staircase in it, a large wide-branched stair leading up either side of the main axis of the space. Thus the hall at Coleshill followed the continental usage as an important room for parade – the vestibule. The great chamber was located as traditionally on the first floor over the great parlour behind the hall. From this scheme, with withdrawing rooms at the

Above: Coleshill House, Oxfordshire, c. 1650–52; Sir Roger Pratt. Destroyed in 1952, this was the quintessential mid-seventeenth-century house

Right: The archetypal 'Double-Pile' plan of Coleshill House with central corridor running the width of the block

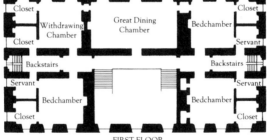

Closet					Closet
Closet	Withdrawing Chamber	Great Dining Chamber		Bedchamber	
					Servant
Backstairs				Backstairs	
Servant					Servant
Bedchamber				Bedchamber	
Closet					Closet

FIRST FLOOR

```
        0  2  4  6  8  10  12  14    m
        0   10   20   30   40   50 ft
→   N
```

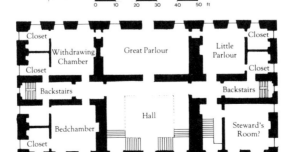

Closet				Little	Closet
Closet	Withdrawing Chamber	Great Parlour		Parlour	Closet
Backstairs				Backstairs	
Bedchamber		Hall		Steward's Room?	
Closet					

GROUND FLOOR

sides of each of these two rooms, it was not far to the full-blooded French plan of a vestibule with a saloon beyond, which seems to have first appeared in England after the Restoration with the return of the Court from the continent. The great hall did not entirely disappear; the screens passage of Jacobean houses, which has been noted as still in use at Raynham Hall, in the 1620s and 1630s, continued to appear in later houses, such as Thorpe Hall (where the main stair actually seems to have run up from the dais end of the hall, an unsurprising archaism.), Tring House, Hertfordshire (now demolished), and Melton Hall, Norfolk, all houses dating from the 1650s to 1680s.

Externally Coleshill was extremely simple. A compact rectangular box, it was raised on a shallow basement storey; its only articulation was by differentiating the storeys, stone-quoins and a heavy cornice, the central axis marked by the wider spacing of the middle bays and the segmentally pedimented entrance. The roof, with its dormers sporting alternating triangular and segmental pediments, was flat topped with a balustrade and a cupola slightly taller than the great chimneys. The interior showed more the direct influence of Jones, with very correct doorcases and the typical, though rather too ornate, ribbed ceilings. The smaller Stuart house was derived from the example of this house, via a number of similar ones, to spread all over the country.

Tredegar Park, Gwent, 1664–74. Another example of a post-Restoration house with surviving cross-windows

Belton House, Lincs, 1685–88; attributed to William Winde. Typical post-Restoration house in stone with wings

The most apt division between the various types of houses common after the Restoration is that invented by Summerson, categorising post-Restoration country houses into three basic types: those with short wings, those with longer wings and those, like Coleshill, without wings. The prototype for the first important type was Clarendon House in London, built by Pratt between 1664 and 1667, which because of its town position will be considered in greater detail in the chapter on town houses. It was the prototype for patrons who required a grander house than Coleshill, with its greater width, its central pediment and its short wings. Pratt repeated the scheme, with rather longer wings, at Holme Lacy in Hereford and Worcester (1674), while other examples included Combe Abbey in Warwickshire by William Winde (1684), Belton House, Lincolnshire (1685–88), and Hanbury Hall, Hereford and Worcester (c. 1701).

Belton House, probably designed by the mason William Stanton, still retains much of its original interior decoration

which is typical of the kind of decoration that would have been found in the more sumptuous house of this date. The plasterwork of the ceilings remains very much in the Jones tradition, and in the staircase, the saloon and the chapel, ribs cut away in the form of floral and leaf decoration produce geometric patterns around the centre of the ceiling while the corners of the space are filled with more leaf squirls, small paintings (as at Sudbury Hall), small mythical scenes or trophies. At Belton it is particularly interesting to see the retention of so much of the original wall-panelling. This is a survival from Jacobean times, when the practice of covering the walls with wood was common, but instead of the repetitive panelling of the linen-fold type so popular then, Belton shows the characteristic post-Restoration form, made up of simple rectangular fielded panels. The saloon at Belton is the most magnificent panelled room in the house, the doors topped by segmental pediments and the overdoors filled with carved swags, as is the panel above the fireplace.

Belton House, Lincs, 1685–88. Saloon, with fielded panelling and very fine carving

32

Although the use of wings in this group of houses was specifically derived from the prototype of Clarendon House, the second basic type kept wings in a hangover from Jacobean times. This is especially true of Ham House in Surrey, where the form was stipulated because it was a conversion of about 1674 by the Earl of Lauderdale of a house originally built in 1610. Another transitional example is Sudbury Hall in Derbyshire, built between 1660 and 1680, with its references both to the present and to the past (see Chapter 1).

The last important type of post-Restoration country house was the most numerous and the most clearly based on Coleshill as well as on the two houses that Hugh May developed from it, Eltham Lodge, Kent (1663–64), and Berkeley House, Piccadilly (1664–66). This type became popular not only as the ideal for the small country house but also because it was superbly suited as a large detached house for the town. In both guises it appeared all over the country, and even in overseas colonies, given great charm by the immense adaptability of the type for most building materials (indeed, in New England houses of this type were often built of wood). Most examples in England were of two storeys and though the characteristic form was therefore fairly low and horizontal, one glorious exception was built, Ashdown House in Oxfordshire (c. 1665), a very tall three-storey hunting-box with balustraded roof and cupola, giving a very good vantage point atop the Berkshire Downs.

Ashdown House, Oxfordshire, c. 1665. Hunting-box of dressed chalk with stone quoins

The Scots did not build country houses before the Restoration, the landed classes living in L or Z plan tower-houses, the local brand of castle, owing to the continuing feudal nature of the country. They were not susceptible to symmetry, but after 1600 a few were given symmetrical wings, such as Pitreavie in Fife (after 1631), or were built with more regular fenestration, as at Muchalls House, Grampian (1619–27), or Innes House, Grampian (William Aytoun, 1640–53). Otherwise the Renaissance had little effect. There were some intimations, particularly in the use of steeply sloping pediments over windows, but otherwise it was not until long after William Wallace had become King's Master-mason in 1617 that any notice was taken of developments other than native. His most important contribution to Scottish architecture was not in any particular building but rather in a widening of the sources for decoration and ideas.

Heriot's Hospital, Edinburgh, begun 1628; William Wallace, William Aytoun and John Mylne. Interior of courtyard showing symmetrification of Scottish tower-house tradition under European influence

Square courtyard plan of Heriot's Hospital derived from France and Germany

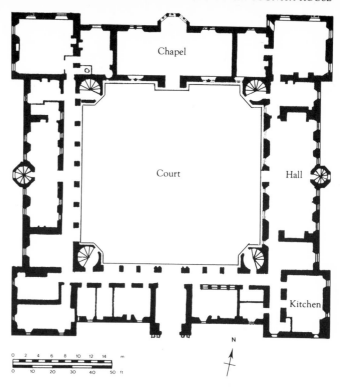

Chapel

Court

Hall

Kitchen

N

He readily used Flemish ornament, such as in his additions to Linlithgow palace (c. 1619–20) or at Wintoun House (completed 1620), but he also set the fashion for increased borrowing of English motifs. His greatest building was Heriot's Hospital in Edinburgh (begun in 1628), and although the square courtyard plan with spiral staircases in the angles seems to have been produced by an English mason for the Chief Overseer, Dr Walter Balcanquall, Dean of Rochester and later of Durham, in about 1627, the major part of the design was left to Wallace. It is not actually the first Scottish example of a building with an English-type plan – this being Barnes Castle, built before 1594, using a plan with wings – but it was to provide a fertile source of motifs for Scottish architecture for several decades. It is very much a hybrid, with quotations from earlier Scottish buildings, Gothic (the chapel exterior), French and Italian (the plan), Jacobean and Flemish. It is the first Scottish building that can be called Classical in spirit, even if that Classicism tends to melt away when the Hospital is examined in detail.

Heriot's Hospital founded a tradition that had its greatest expression in Drumlanrig Castle, Dumfries and Galloway, built for the Duke of Queensberry between 1675 and 1689: in many ways this is extremely simple – a courtyard plan with a loggia, corner towers, turrets, steeply sloping pediments and the continued use of Gothic – but Classical ornament is more in evidence, particularly in the magnificent applied Corinthian order of the entrance-front. Classicism as a way of building for Scottish noblemen had become unavoidable; in 1671 Charles II appointed Sir William Bruce as Surveyor-General for Scotland. As a minor nobleman of some importance he was a supporter of the Restoration, as indeed was Scotland generally. Bruce's early work was modest enough, concentrating on the symmetricalisation of older houses such as Balcaskie, Fife; his first essay in a Classical style of European quality was the renovation of the Palace of Holyroodhouse, carried out to provide accommodation for the king in his other kingdom. Although Bruce retained older parts and made the whole symmetrical, the interior of the courtyard is much more contemporary than anything else built in Scotland at this time.

Above: Drumlanrig Castle, Dumfries and Galloway, c. 1675–90; James Smith to the designs of Robert Mylne. The west front retains the height of the tower-house tradition

The entrance front of Drumlanrig Castle, with still rather crude monumental centre following fashion

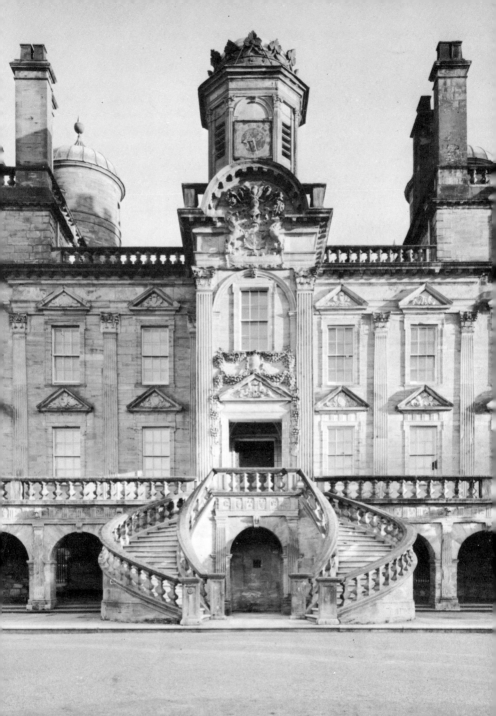

Around the courtyard he arrayed ranges that were very simple but also French in feel, with an arcaded ground floor, each side articulated by a continuous Doric order on the ground floor, by Ionic on the first and by Corinthian on the second. Not an inspired design, it nevertheless shows the competence with which Bruce could handle Classicism.

Left: Palace of Holyroodhouse, Edinburgh, 1671–79; altered by Sir William Bruce. Interior of the court with shallow articulation in the manner of French seventeenth-century Classicism

Right: Hopetoun House, Lothian, 1699–1703; Sir William Bruce. The garden side is all that remains of the exterior after remodelling by the Adams

Kinross House, Tayside (1686–93), was Bruce's masterpiece. Owing something to Pratt in its plan (double-pile like Coleshill) and in its compactness, though it is a larger house, and in its exterior design to houses like Ashburnham House in Westminster, it is articulated by pilasters instead of the more normal quoins. The interior is decorated similarly to Holyroodhouse, with a beautiful entrance hall with freestanding columns. In 1699 Bruce began Hopetoun House, Lothian. It has since become famous, not only because of William Adam's not unworthy alterations (1723–48), but also because it was the scene of some of Robert and John Adam's first works (1750–56). The garden façade is the only one left much as originally, but it has become swamped by the rest of the work. The most exciting Bruce remnant is the octagonal stairwell, with fretwork of decorated wood-panelling moving through squinches to an octagonal cupola.

Kinross House, Tayside, 1686–93; Sir William Bruce. Garden front of Bruce's masterpiece

After 1700 these types of smaller houses began to be replaced, in England by the baroque and in Scotland by the characteristic, rather French Palladianism introduced by Bruce, both of which will be described in the next chapter. The Restoration house remains in many ways the quintessence of the English country house, and its modesty, serenity and dignity without pomposity recommended it as a basis for the establishment of a truly English style among Edwardian architects of the Queen Anne and neo-baroque movements at the end of the last century.

3

THE BAROQUE
COUNTRY HOUSE

All of the houses mentioned in the last chapter were moderate in size, and none could compare in splendour with the great houses of the Elizabethan or Jacobean eras, with the exception of the Palace of Holyroodhouse. Around 1680, however, a remarkable transformation began, given impetus by the influence of continental developments and by the increasing power of the aristocracy vis-à-vis the Crown that was to lead to the great Whig country houses of the late seventeenth and early eighteenth centuries. In 1660 Louis XIV assumed personal rule in France and began work on the refitting of the Louvre in Paris. Later in the decade he embarked on the rebuilding of Versailles, a task that was to prove of great moment for the designing of larger houses in Europe and was to have its reflection in Britain.

The earliest example of this French style in England is to be seen in the suites added at Windsor designed by Hugh May between 1674 and 1684. To the exteriors May gave crenellations and deep arched windows, an early example of the English baroque concern with medieval architecture. The interior was much more baroque, organised around two staircases as in earlier houses (such as Hatfield House); the palace was divided into two separate, though connected, 'sides', one for the king and one for the queen, each, as was the established continental fashion, a succession of rooms with precise functions. These varied from country to country and house to house in number, order and use; on the king's side at Windsor, at the top of the staircase were found guard-chamber, audience-chamber and the more private rooms of the withdrawing chamber, bed-chamber and closet. As Mark Girouard has shown, the higher one's status the further along

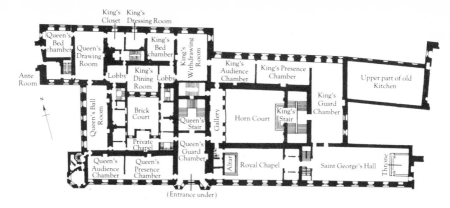

King's Closet
King's Dressing Room
Queen's Bed chamber
Queen's Drawing Room
King's Bed chamber
King's Withdrawing Room
King's Audience Chamber
King's Presence Chamber
Upper part of old Kitchen
Ante Room
Lobby
King's Dining Room
Lobby
King's Guard Chamber
Queen's Ball Room
Brick Court
Queen's Stair
Gallery
Horn Court
King's Stair
N
Private Chapel
Queen's Guard Chamber
Queen's Audience Chamber
Queen's Presence Chamber
Altar
Royal Chapel
Saint George's Hall
Throne
(Entrance under)

Windsor Castle, Upper Ward, Berkshire, after 1674; Hugh May. The first English palace plan to show the influence of the French *appartement*

the line one was able to penetrate, and in a hierarchical, status-conscious age, systems of this kind were important throughout Europe. (In Scotland Holyroodhouse was refurbished in one of the most outspoken of French exterior styles, while the interior was organised in the French manner.) Both the king's and queen's sides at Windsor were decorated in lavish fashion by the Italian illusionist painter, Antonio Verrio, the gilder Cousin, and the carver and sculptor Grinling Gibbons. The decoration was intended as a direct demonstration of the power and magnificence of the Crown, using various subjects taken from ancient mythology with Charles II and Catherine of Braganza appearing in many scenes. The most spectacular rooms were St George's Hall (1682–84) and the Royal Chapel (1680–84), both large and decorated almost entirely by illusionist painting, with large scenes divided by a fictional painted architectural framework. Both these rooms

St George's Hall, Windsor Castle, 1682–84; Hugh May. View of the Hall as decorated by Antonio Verrio from W. H. Pyne's 'Royal Residences' of 1819 (destroyed)

have disappeared, but they were to be of great importance to the designing of grand interiors later in the century.

Windsor and the Palace of Holyroodhouse were the only works completed by Charles II. Earlier, John Webb had begun to rebuild Greenwich Palace (1664), but by 1669 when work stopped only the so-called King Charles block had been completed. As a composition the block is rather overstated, owing to Webb's intention of a larger palace with a domed central block which was not built. Even so, the block is normally described as the first baroque building in Britain because of its simple, direct, monumental appearance, its main vertical accents of portico and end-pavilions connected by extremely bold string-courses across the wings. It provided an obvious precedent of quality for the building of the rest of the palace as a hospital during the 1690s. Charles II's other plan was for a palace at Winchester, begun in 1678 to Wren's designs but left unfinished in 1685 at the accession of James II. With its long court, with extruded corners, leading back to a hexastyle portico and domed saloon, it was extremely French in style (following Versailles) and looked forward to Hampton Court, Wren's most complete surviving essay in palace-building.

Having decided to rebuild the palace at Hampton Court King William III and Queen Mary received from Wren with great dispatch two huge projects for rebuilding this palace inherited from Wolsey and Henry VIII, plus a third not so ambitious, only proposing two ranges, which was accepted. The two wings were divided between the customary king and

King Charles Block, Greenwich Palace (now Hospital), 1664–69; John Webb. Palladian block with monumental baroque stress on centre and ends

Hampton Court
Palace, Richmond-
upon-Thames,
1689–95; Sir
Christopher
Wren. Wren's
largest surviving
palace combining
French and Dutch
influences

queen's sides, the king's enfilade overlooking the Privy
Garden and the queen's the Great Fountain Garden. The order
of the rooms was much the same as at Windsor with smaller
rooms, corridors and galleries overlooking the Fountain
Court behind. Most of the old Tudor Palace was left
untouched although Wren did add a colonnade at the south
end of the Clock Court to provide sheltered passage for
visitors to the king's staircase at the entrance to his apartment.
Interior decoration was of much the same order as at Windsor,
though the scheme was never completed, with iconographical
references to the king and queen being found on ceilings and
walls all through the block, as well as references to Queen Anne
who continued the decoration.

The exterior has much the same air of quiet tension that
Wren created with such great effect at St Paul's. Details
referring to Versailles – such as the attached orders in the
middle of both fronts and the lack of depth to the façades – are
not surprising, but the general effect is standard Wren.
Hampton Court, in its quiet English way, is in many ways the
post-restoration country house writ large. The use of brick on
such a large scale has been censured, but it did allow greater
crowding of motifs than stone while leading to an overall effect
that is one of serenity and, more important, cheaper and
quicker to build, points of significance for William.

As one might expect, French influence on exteriors seems
to have been a specific importation. Ralph Montagu, later
Duke of Montagu, had been English Ambassador in France.
He was well-known for his French tastes, and his London

house, Montagu House, had separate roofs over the pavilions at the ends of the block, as well as interior decoration carried out by Frenchmen. At Boughton, his country seat in Northamptonshire, he added a block not only painted inside by the Frenchman, Louis Chéron, and filled with his great collection of French furniture, but also planned 'en enfilade' leading from staircase to bedroom (with the doors to each room all lined up). The exterior, with its ground-floor banded rusticated arcade, flat first-floor pilaster order and mansard roof, was the most French-looking at this time (c. 1690–94), rivalled only by Petworth, Sussex (c. 1688–90), with its very French restraint and very precise articulation and detail, which seems to have originally sported a central dome, burned down in a fire in 1714 and never replaced.

Boughton House, Northamptonshire, begun 1688. The French appearance is comparable to that of Holyroodhouse

Whereas both Boughton and Petworth followed the French example in the use of the 'enfilade', this was never common outside palace design, British country-house planning following its own separate tradition. At Coleshill the rooms on the central axis were the most important ones – the hall, the great parlour beyond and, upstairs, the great dining chamber. At Ragley Hall, Warwickshire, designed twenty-eight years later, the parlour and dining chamber were combined in function as the saloon beyond the hall, and the four corners of the block were taken up with apartments, much smaller than

Ragley Hall,
Warwickshire,
1679–83; Robert
Hooke. A large
house with double
depth centre and
apartments in the
corners

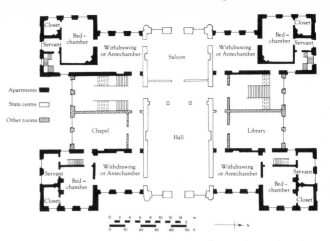

the French practice, made up of the traditional antechamber,
bed-chamber and closet. Although Ragley was a large house
for its time, it was, compared with Chatsworth, Castle Howard
or Blenheim, fairly compact, and it provided a standard by
which other later houses could be organised. Often, as at
Heythrop or Kings Weston in Avon later, the house was made
even more compact by placing the apartments along the sides
of the state-centre axis rather than perpendicular to it, as at
Castle Howard or Blenheim. The rare use of the grandest type
of organisation was due to the lack of noblemen who were able
to build in this way, most of the builders of country houses
being gentlemen or minor nobility without the income, the
political power, or indeed the inclination to match the Duke of
Devonshire or the Earl of Carlisle.

The baroque, although partially present, as mentioned earlier,
in the King Charles block at Greenwich, was first seen fully-
fledged in William Talman's south front at Chatsworth
(1687–89, for the Duke of Devonshire), a monumental
twelve-bay wide elevation, the centre recessed, the three end
bays to either side articulated by a giant, partly fluted, Ionic
order, and with giant keystones over the windows, all topped
by a very heavy cornice, parapet and roof-top balustrade
carrying urns. It is interesting that forms become heavier
towards the sky-line, adding greatly to the monumental
presence of the building. The use of pilasters to articulate the
ends of the block and the heavy keystones probably derive
from the Greenwich wing. However, the assertive emotional
impact of this front is far greater than Webb's block and is
the first true example of the baroque in Britain.

In date the Talman Chatsworth front stands rather alone. The next block to be begun there, the west wing (possibly by Thomas Archer), dates from 1700, twelve years after the south front, and combines the same basic rhythms of the Talman façade with the addition of an attached portico and pediment. Talman himself does not seem to have matched the strength of his Chatsworth façade in any other building, the entrance front at Dyrham Park in Avon, an addition to an earlier house, dated 1700, being the nearest approach though lacking the forceful use of both keystones and giant order. Dyrham's is also similar to the long and gaunt entrance front of Burley-on-the-Hill, Leicestershire (1694–c. 1700), a palatial house that stands, rather like Ragley Hall, in the no-man's-land between the smaller Stuart-type of country house and the more massive baroque house. Talman was also responsible for the unique additions to the old house at Drayton, Northamptonshire, including the one-storey hall-front on the north-side of the court, a strange confection in a style that has its roots both in French seventeenth-century Classicism and Flemish seventeenth-century mannerism and has little to do with the baroque.

The massive four-square block, with or without pilasters but with horizontal emphasis given by a cornice or parapet at roof-level, was a house-type that was to become popular. Blocks became much taller and with a heavier cornice combined monumentality and compactness. Most of the houses in this

Chatsworth House, Derbyshire, 1687–96; William Talman. The first true baroque façade in England

group were large, if not actually palatial;stone, also, was much more common as the building material of this type of house compared to the Stuart country house. The greatest offspring of Talman's Chatsworth façade is Heythrop, a house in Oxfordshire begun c. 1707 by Thomas Archer. Increased emphasis is given to the block by the use of columns, itself rare in a house of this period, and by the heavy cornice and balustrade, fully the height of one storey of the house. A later and beautiful example of this type of larger baroque house is the now ruined Sutton Scarsdale of 1724, in Derbyshire not far from Chatsworth. It is an astonishing house built, during a time when Palladian ideas were taking root, by Francis Smith, a builder of Warwick. With its fully rusticated walls it seems to look back to Greenwich sixty years earlier, while nodding at more sophisticated palace architecture in France and Germany. It is an altogether more assured essay than Smith's earlier house, Stoneleigh Abbey, Warwickshire (begun in 1714). Another house of this rather flat type is Wentworth Castle in South Yorkshire, built between 1710 and 1714. The south front is a rather special case which, although locking perfectly into the development of the English house at this time, seems to have been based on a design of Jean de Bodt, an architect resident in north-east Germany, later to become superintendent of building in Dresden. Its use of restraint as a positive factor as well as the round-arched centre-piece signifies the extent to which French values were coming to the fore.

Sutton Scarsdale, Derbyshire, begun 1724; Francis Smith's most splendid house, now unfortunately a ruin

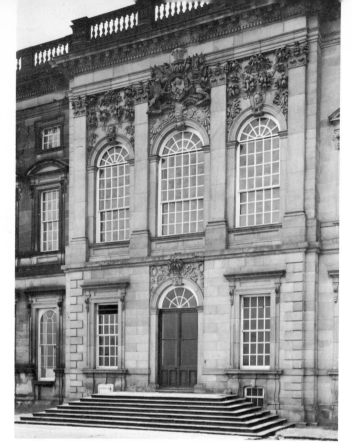

Wentworth Castle, South Yorkshire, c. 1710–20; Jean de Bodt. Centre of façade showing lavish decorational stonework

The massiveness that is one of the key-notes of the baroque country house can nowhere be seen to better advantage than in the work of Hawksmoor and Vanbrugh. At Easton Neston, Northamptonshire (1696/97–1702), the only important house entirely by Wren's pupil and assistant Nicholas Hawksmoor, the emphasis was again on giving a not overlarge block extra monumentality, and again this was achieved by the use of simple and plain forms, such as the massive cornice supported by a giant Corinthian order. Both façades are built up by layers of the order, a complexity typical of Hawksmoor who had the necessary ability and knowledge of Classicism to transcend its inherent discipline and use it for entirely novel effects, such as the combination of two- and four-storey fenestration schemes within the one façade on the north front.

For the grand, the massive and the unexpected in the architecture of the country house at this period, one architect stands out, Sir John Vanbrugh. An architect whose personal style was one of the most individual in the whole history of

Easton Neston,
Northamptonshire,
1696/97–1702;
Nicholas
Hawksmoor.
Above: East façade,
with highly
complicated
articulation adding
monumentality to
relatively small
house

Right: North
façade, the use of
two fenestration
schemes showing
that the exterior
might be a shell
surrounding an
earlier house

English architecture, he dominates the history of country house building after the turn of the century.

Even Vanbrugh's entry onto the architectural stage was unexpected. Dean Swift wrote:

> 'Van's Genius without Thought or Lecture,
> Is Hugely turnd to Architecture.'

The words to be emphasised in that couplet are 'Genius' and 'Hugely'; there is no doubt that to contemporaries he cut a larger-than-life figure. It is that which impresses us today.

Vanbrugh had, by the late 1690s, led a varied and interesting life as a commissioned officer in the army who had been imprisoned in France, and he had subsequently taken to writing those extremely complex and, to us, salacious comedies then fashionable. Vanbrugh has always seemed a sympathetic figure because like the heroes of pre-war thrillers it seems that he was able in whatever task he turned his hand to. This has even been taken as evidence for frivolity of character, and thus when he 'hugely turnd to Architecture', how could it be otherwise than as a new fad or perhaps an elegant piece of waggishness? It is not possible to isolate this trait in his character, for he was undoubtedly good company and, as a member of the Kit-Kat Club of Whig grandees, regarded as the social equal of many of his patrons. However, about architecture Vanbrugh was extremely serious.

Vanbrugh's first demonstration of interest in architecture is one of the more curious in the history of the subject. In 1698 the Earl of Carlisle had decided to build and had engaged William Talman, a difficult man later dismissed as too expensive (Talman always insisted on using his own men at London rates of pay). Vanbrugh was then engaged, designs were made and in late 1699 the house – more of a country palace, in fact – was begun.

It does not seem that Vanbrugh was architecturally illiterate, but an interest in buildings and the actual design and building of a house the size of Castle Howard are two quite different things, and he therefore needed assistance. This he found in Hawksmoor, not only a capable organiser and a skilled draughtsman, but an individual designer who brought to the partnership ideas that Vanbrugh found much to his liking. How they met and how they got along are not known, but when Vanbrugh felt able to pursue his own course after Blenheim they remained firm friends. And it is surely too much to ask that Hawksmoor, a proud man, and in architectural terms at least a perfectionist, would have had any truck with a buffoon or an architectural charlatan.

In Vanbrugh's first two houses, therefore, the hand of Hawksmoor is evident. Castle Howard, North Yorkshire, built between 1699 and 1710, is Vanbrugh's most traditional building, and although the courtyard façade, with its rhythmic grouping of paired pilasters on the main block and overall

Castle Howard, North Yorkshire, 1699–1726; Sir John Vanbrugh. The French influence on Vanbrugh before his development of a more personal idiom

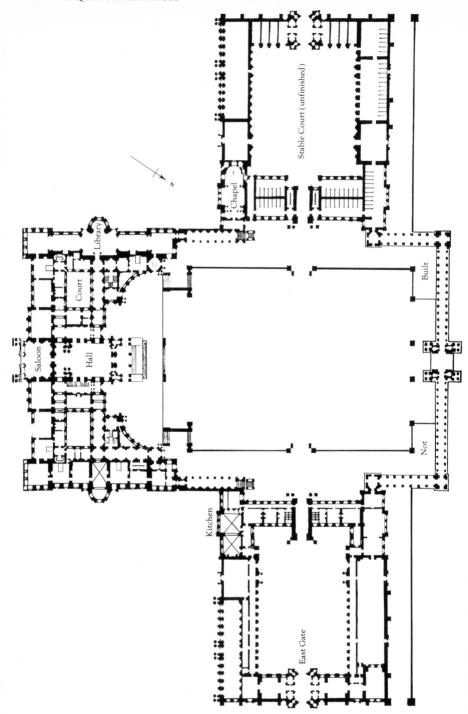

Left: Blenheim Palace, Oxfordshire, 1705–16; Sir John Vanbrugh. One of the very few British house plans that approach Versailles in scope

Below: Garden façade of Blenheim Palace, with massive central block and corner towers with 'eminencies'

rustication, shows the shape of things to come, the rich and splendid garden-façade is as characteristic a piece of palace spectacular as can be found in any country in Europe. The cupola, although topping-off the composition, is rather clumsily placed, but otherwise the design is well conceived. The magnificence of the interior is matched by the domed hall inside, top-lit from the cupola and decorated with the paintings *The Fall of Phaeton* and *The Four Elements* by Pellegrini (1709–12), visible from and looking into the staircases at either side. The plan, otherwise, is not especially complicated, derived from Palladio via French houses of the mid-seventeenth century. The most interesting feature is the way that an enclosed court is formed on the entrance side by wings swinging round from the sides of the hall (only built to Vanbrugh's design on the left), while the rooms on the garden side form two straight wings either side of the saloon. Very much the same plan was used at Blenheim, though on a larger scale and with the addition of two extra wings to close off the sides between court and garden-side wings.

Had Vanbrugh not built anything more he would have been known as the designer of one of the greatest of English country houses. He would also be known as a much more continentally inspired architect than he was to be in practice. Blenheim Palace (1705–16) trounced Castle Howard in one blow. The comparison, though natural, is invidious, however, for whereas Castle Howard is a large, even palatial, country house, Blenheim was intended as a monument to the victory of the British and Austrian armies over the French at the Battle of Blenheim in 1704, in the form of a house for the architect of that victory, the Duke of Marlborough. Blenheim was therefore intended as a monument national, even international in scope.

Although Castle Howard gives a substantial idea of Vanbrugh's capabilities, particularly in the entrance front and the splendour of the Hall, it is at Blenheim that the main elements of his style first appear. The entrance-court view of

Hall of Blenheim Palace, probably by Nicholas Hawksmoor, harking back to the medieval conception with its function for the grandest banquets

the house 'where every piece of the architect's motley ordnance is manned and the whole battery is fired at you at once', in Kerry Downes's words, is of a complexity that contrasts both with the garden-front and with the entrance-front at Castle Howard. The division of responsibility between Vanbrugh and Hawksmoor is, again, not easy to discern, but the power and emotion are Vanbrugh's, Hawksmoor only adding the necessary refinement.

The house was built to the same basic plan as Castle Howard, with the central axis taken up by the hall and saloon, and with two apartments spreading either side of the saloon along the garden front, while a private apartment is positioned in the west wing and a long library in the east. The main entrance is recessed into the block, and the outer court formed by the blocks of kitchen and stable courts (the latter unfinished) to either side. Recession, one of the prerequisites of baroque planning, is increased by the continuous interweaving of motifs through the composition. The main elements, the central block and the pair of rusticated and seemingly embattled corner towers (repeating a motif of the garden-side), are linked by curving colonnades that disappear into the two towers only to reappear to link the towers to the service court blocks. The porticoed central block, given added emphasis by a clerestory that is a recessed temple, is taller than the main body of the house. The attached portico and paired half-columns to either side, fluted and Corinthian, speak of martial might and Apollonian splendour and exude the impression of this house as a national monument.

At Blenheim Vanbrugh's obsession with the broken outline of a building appears for the first time. This manifests itself not only in the projection and recession of the plan but also, and more prominently, in the use of roof-top towers and 'eminencies' to add interest to the skyline of a building. There has been much speculation as to the genesis of the extraordinary roof projections, the so-called 'eminencies', and comparisons with Elizabethan 'prodigy' houses such as Wollaton, with their varied roof-lines, have been made. Vanbrugh regarded the 'castle air' as most important, but it is achieved at Blenheim with towers of such a level of sophistication compared to his later buildings that it is very improbable that he was responsible for the detailed design of them.

The hall was probably designed by Hawksmoor; a very tall clerestoried space flanked by two staircases visible through

two-storeyed arcades, and with a heavily moulded cornice supported by a giant Corinthian order, it demonstrates the route to the saloon by a huge proscenium arch. The saloon, with its extraordinary white-marble recessed doorcases by Hawksmoor and Gibbons (who had carved the capitals in the hall), was decorated by Laguerre (1719–20), with an apotheosis on the ceiling and illusionistic architecture round the walls, framing representatives of the four continents.

In 1710–11 the return of a Tory government led to the disgrace of Marlborough and the stoppage of funds; Vanbrugh was dismissed by the Duchess, Sarah, and things ticked over until 1722, when Hawksmoor was recalled to finish the interior. Unfortunately the rooms of the south front were later redecorated in the rococo style (1905), though happily the ceilings to the east of the saloon were retained, as was the extraordinary tripartite decoration of the long library (1722–25).

Vanbrugh's later houses were built without Hawksmoor's involvement, and they show a primitive streak not apparent at Castle Howard or Blenheim – the 'castle air' writ large. Monumentality was assured by the almost total rejection of detail, and Vanbrugh explored the minimal use of heavy string-courses, key-stones and window-mouldings (indeed, in some cases the omission of those mouldings altogether), the common use of unadorned arcades and towers (especially

Seaton Delaval, Northumberland, 1720–28; Sir John Vanbrugh. Plainer than Castle Howard and Blenheim Palace but with more emphatic use of detail

arcaded chimney towers), and of crenellations and machicolations. Vanbrugh, like Hawksmoor, even turned to the use of the Gothic, but rather for emotional impact than for any archaeological or intellectual reasons.

At Kimbolton, Cambridgeshire, Vanbrugh recased an earlier courtyard house (1707–19). Simple and bold, with his first use of battlements, the house was later (c. 1719) given a large and rather staring portico by the Roman late baroque architect Allessandro Galilei. Kings Weston in Avon (1712–14) is far more original, a squarish block with projections on three fronts and a deep recession on the north. It shows the primitive nature of the path that Vanbrugh was following. Even the pilastered portico of the entrance front is rendered simply in stone of the same kind as the wall, giving an air of abstraction that consorts well with the simple window embrasures and the heavy moulding of string-courses and roof-parapet.

The dramatic force of this style could be increased by the use of rustication and heavy banded window surrounds as at Seaton Delaval, Northumberland (1720–28) and Eastbury, Dorset (c. 1718–38; now destroyed). Vanbrugh's use of architectural detail was due to his realisation that the order, and most forms of decoration, were of greatest significance in increasing the emotional force of buildings when used sparingly and with care. To quote Downes once more: 'Having found that mere mass and void could speak, he used an order, preferably full columns, for giant punches of the highest drama'. Thus at Seaton Delaval, perhaps Vanbrugh's most evocative house, he uses a large balustraded portico on the garden front, while the order on the north front is restricted to paired columns on either side of the entrance. With short octagonal towers at each corner of the block, two taller square stair-towers at each side and the re-emergence of the Blenheim-like pitched roof clerestory surmounting all, the house presents an extraordinarily dramatic profile unmatched by any buildings of the period on the continent. The hall (gutted in 1822), is arcaded on all sides, similarly to the much larger hall at Grimsthorpe, Lincolnshire, where, as at Castle Howard and Blenheim, the staircases are placed to each side of the central axis.

Grimsthorpe was Vanbrugh's last building and presents something of a problem because it shows him turning back to a more Classical repertory. It was to have been the complete rebuilding of an earlier courtyard-plan house, but only the

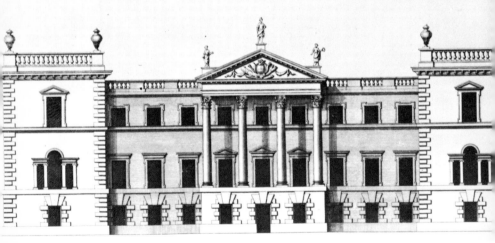

north-facing entrance front was completed. As designed the
unbuilt façade, shown in *Vitruvius Britannicus*, was to have
been much more Palladian than one would have imagined of
Vanbrugh. Indeed, after the massiveness of Eastbury and
Seaton Delaval, even the entrance façade existing today is
surprising, with its low arcaded centre flanked by the typically
Vanbrughian paired banded columns, themselves flanked by a

Left: Grimsthorpe Castle, Lincolnshire, 1722–26; Sir John Vanbrugh. Typical Vanbrughian detail in the centre, with towers influenced by the Italian Renaissance

Below: Unbuilt façade of Grimsthorpe Castle illustrated in *Vitruvius Britannicus*, volume 3, showing interest in Palladian design

pair of towers that display their authorship only in the use of massive keystones over the openings of the low ground storey.

Hawksmoor and, particularly, Vanbrugh were important also in the design of gardens. Advising that the ruin of Woodstock Manor in the park at Blenheim should not be pulled down, Vanbrugh argued that 'it would make one of the most agreeable objects that the best of Landskip painters can invent', evidence of a sensibility that prefigured the Picturesque movement which, later in the century, stressed the importance of buildings in their landscape settings. At Castle Howard Vanbrugh retained the seventeenth-century use of formal avenues and gardens, but used them to astound with the most extraordinary collections of garden buildings in the country, including the Carrmire and Pyramid Gates (both seemingly crude mixtures of motifs from Classical and castle architecture), the Temple of the Four Winds (1725–28), based on Palladio's Villa Rotonda at Vicenza, later to become one of the leitmotifs of Palladianism, an obelisk, a pyramid, several pedestals and urns, and the Mausoleum (1729–36) by Hawksmoor. This last, both the greatest garden ornament as well as the greatest personal funerary monument in Britain, is the burial place of the Howard family. Standing solitary on a rise away from the house, its extraordinarily haunting drama is the product of the serried rank of Roman Doric columns encircling the central chamber and seeming to guard the spirits inside. Its effect is Roman-style Wagnerian, ever-evocative of half-remembered history; its Classicism, which Hawksmoor defended against charges of wilful inaccuracy from Lord Burlington, is one that afterwards could be repeated only in accuracy, not in emotional power.

Most of the houses so far discussed were built for the major nobility. For those not able to afford such splendour there developed a smaller, more provincial baroque house-type. One of the greatest spurs to this was the emergence of a number of masons and builders who had worked with the baroque masters, both in London and on the major country houses (this was also to be important in the development of the post-Wren church – see Chapter 5). Characteristically these smaller houses were of brick with or without stone dressings, with the cornice below the attic rather than at parapet level, supported by angle-pilasters, in a scheme probably derived from William Winde's Buckingham House in London. The

Above: Mawley Hall, Shropshire, 1730; possibly by Francis Smith. A late baroque house in brick with stone dressings, since restored

Left: Head of staircase at Mawley Hall, with plasterwork of Central European quality

Crowcombe Court, Somerset, 1734; Nathaniel Ireson. Provincial baroque house with continental-type detailing

West Midlands where Francis Smith, the designer of Stoneleigh Abbey, Warwickshire, and Sutton Scarsdale, Derbyshire, was active, are particularly rich in these block-like houses, such as, in Shropshire, Cound Hall (1704), Buntingsdale Hall (1721) and Mawley Hall (1730); in Staffordshire, Chillington Hall (1724), Swynnerton Hall (1725) and Swinfen Hall (1755); Compton Verney in Warwickshire (1714); and Pickhill House in Clwyd (1720s). Another group of houses is that in the west country, although it is difficult to name any particular architect as the motive force behind them, for they vary so much in style and quality: for example, Chettle House in Dorset (after 1711), Barnsley Park in Gloucestershire (1720–31), The Ivy, Chippenham in Wiltshire (c. 1727), Widcombe Manor in Bath (c. 1727), and Ven House (c. 1725) and Crowcombe Court in Somerset (1734). In and around Blandford Forum in Dorset, the Bastard family found the type admirably suited to town use, with its flat façades, its usual three storeys and its use of brick with simple but bold articulation. Around London the occurrence of this type is more problematic because few of the houses are quite so typical and none are so easily attributable to one single hand. Cottesbrooke Hall in Northamptonshire (1703–13); Wotton House (1704), Marlow Place (c. 1720), Chicheley House (1720–25), and Iver Grove (1722–24) in Buckinghamshire; Roehampton House (1710–12), Wandsworth, London; Moor Park (c. 1720–28), Hertfordshire; Hawnes Park (c. 1720), Bedfordshire; Hursley Park (c. 1720), Hampshire; and Sudbrooke Lodge (c. 1728), Richmond, London, all show vestiges of the style but the assurance of the architects was great enough for them to be able to stray where others were unwilling or unable to go.

A similar provincial eclecticism can be found in Yorkshire. The influence of Vanbrugh was great, of course, but not as great as might be assumed. The plainness of Duncombe Park, North Yorkshire (begun 1713) by William Wakefield, is one of a number of Vanbrughian motifs normally attributed to that house, but some, including the small tower-like chimneys

Chicheley House, Buckinghamshire, 1720–25; possibly designed by Francis Smith. But the house shows Austrian influence that would have been odd for Smith

Duncombe Park, North Yorkshire, begun 1713; William Wakefield. Yorkshire baroque house perhaps influenced by Vanbrugh

at each end of the garden front, were added by Charles Barry between 1843 and 1846. On that façade typical baroque placing of pilasters is combined with clumsy massing entirely untypical of Vanbrugh. The entrance façade, plain and with a pedimented portico, all set on a basement, sails extremely close to Palladianism. Vanbrugh was later to turn to a near variant of the style at Grimsthorpe, and it had been used around the country since the turn of the century (especially in Oxford); this façade was not an isolated phenomenon in its time. Wakefield's later design for Atherton Hall (1723, not built), with rusticated basement and attached portico, was an essay in the same style, now to be seen in the light of contemporary Palladian practice, while Farfield Hall, North Yorkshire (1728), by virtue of the large parapet and lack of basement, looks rather old-fashioned. This perhaps rather surprising attachment to plain exteriors is most obvious in Bramham Park, West Yorkshire (possibly by Lord Bingley himself, c. 1705–10), and in the court-façade of Gilling Castle, North Yorkshire (probably by Wakefield, after 1719), two houses the plainness of which is emphasised by their use of ashlar and their (curiously for this period) horizontal aspect.

Beningborough Hall, North Yorkshire, before 1716. Monumental house with interesting baroque detail

The similarity of Beningborough Hall, North Yorkshire (before 1716), a two-storey block with heavy banded quoins and a deep cornice supported on doubled brackets, to houses around London and in the West Midlands has led it to be attributed to Thomas Archer, among others; however, it is singular enough for it to have been the work of some local architect.

Bruce founded a school of English-influenced country house design in Scotland and was followed by two architects, James Smith and Alexander McGill, whose styles were based on his and who produced a number of high quality, if rather unenterprising, houses. Plain regular houses with pedimented centre-pieces, such as Melville House, Fife, by Smith (1697–1700), became standard, even for smaller houses, between 1690 and 1715. Wren and Hooke were important influences, as was French house-design. Hamilton Palace by Smith (c. 1693–1701; now demolished), the remodelling of an existing house, was very like Ragley, as is Dalkeith House, Lothian (1702–11), the regularisation of a medieval (and later) castle, the court façade an exercise in recession and play in roof-planes, very much in the Wren–Hooke tradition. This unassuming type of house continued to be built, though the tradition was partially broken by the advent of the maverick William Adam.

It is one of the more interesting little questions of architectural history whether Adam was an architect of great flair and knowledge who used the architectural vocabulary in a novel and interesting way or a provincial builder with little understanding who, by luck rather than finesse, produced some excitingly fresh houses. The east front of Hopetoun House, Lothian (enlarged 1723–48), Adam's largest com-

Hopetoun House, Lothian, entrance façade enlarged 1723–48; William Adam and, later, Robert and John Adam. The most palatial façade in Scotland

position and his only work in a palace style, is the stateliest of his houses with a giant Corinthian pilaster order and concave transitions to the wings, a building with an intelligent use of motifs from France, Wren and even Vanbrugh. Duff House, Grampian (1735–39), Adam's other monumental composition, has been seen as a provincial re-interpretation of motifs from Castle Howard, particularly in its use of a pedimented Corinthian centre-piece, but that use of the Corinthian order and towers makes it also an interesting paraphrase of Drumlanrig Castle. Adam was never a Palladian, and his eclectic use of motifs from many styles and the refusal of his buildings to fall into any logical stylistic progression make him, in many ways, as characteristic a product of the late baroque as any architect in these islands, indeed in his provinciality closer to some of the architects of the Central European baroque.

The country house was in England the most characteristic of baroque building types. As a style the baroque was, like Elizabethan and the later Victorian Italianate Classicism, superbly adapted to demonstrate the personal power of clients and patrons. However, it was by no means a universal style; as mentioned in Chapter 2 the more modest Stuart and Restoration country house type continued to be built throughout the baroque period and adapted itself quickly to Palladianism. In Scotland and in the general area of town-house building it was relatively unimportant. With the exception of Greenwich Hospital, it was only in church-building, particularly the works of Hawksmoor and Archer, that the baroque country house finds a parallel in other building types.

4

TOWN AND VERNACULAR HOUSES

By contrast with the countries of continental Europe Britain has no tradition of town-palace building, except in the specific case of the sovereign, in either England or Scotland. Whereas in Italy the building of palaces by the powerful had been a principle means for the new style of the Renaissance to take hold and spread, a sequence to be followed by France and Central Europe in the seventeenth century, in Britain the town-palace was to be of only small importance, and there were certainly none that could be compared in size or magnificence with the greatest in Rome, Venice, Paris, Vienna, Munich or Berlin. In part this was a reflection of the different constitutional background of Britain, travelling in the seventeenth century a very different path from continental absolutism, but it was also a reflection of both the less centralised aspect of the hierarchy of British society and the greater importance that classes other than the nobility played in the prosperity of the nation. It was also a question of tradition; during the reigns of Elizabeth and James I London had been the undisputed seat of the Court, and the nobility had faced far less competition in the shires.

Without the impetus of palace-building, what was the course of activity in the towns? The British town house of the later seventeenth century was the product of the amalgamation of three distinct streams of development: the timber house, the Jonesian house and the large mid-century London town houses. Timber houses of the Jacobean era with timber frames and jettied fronts were built right through the Commonwealth and, in the provinces indeed, almost until the turn of the century. However, at a time of increasing living standards (and with the examples of disastrous fires destroying towns with a high prevalence of timber and timber-framed houses), where brick and stone supplies were plentiful, these materials were becoming more common, usually employed in the artisan style, with the typical scrolled and pedimented gables and in some cases canted bays containing windows. This tradition lasted even longer, remaining popular in some less accessible parts of the kingdom into the following century.

Around 1640, in Great Queen Street and Lincoln's Inn Fields, London (Lindsey House, still surviving) houses were treated for the first time in what was thought to be a more Classical style. The impetus for this would seem to have been the Classicism of Jones, as manifested in a group of contemporary, though awkward-looking houses, all influenced by Jones, such as Baulm's House, Hackney, and Lees Court, Kent, in combination with the influence of France. In 1631–37 Covent Garden had been rebuilt, again with houses united behind a single façade (as in Great Queen Street), on two sides of the Piazza (a Victorian reconstruction of part survives on the north side of the present Covent

Lindsey House, Lincoln's Inn Fields, London, c. 1640; possibly by Nicholas Stone. Among the first houses to be treated in a Classical way

Garden). Although Jones supervised the project for the Earl of Bedford and designed the church, it has been assumed that these blocks were the work of a Frenchman, Isaac de Caus, who would have had knowledge of recent French developments. In the early part of the century in Paris, especially in the Place Dauphine and the Place des Vosges, houses of a lesser status than the Parisian *hôtel particulier* (town-palace) had been united behind a common façade, and the blocks at Covent Garden are indebted to the Place des Vosges, with its arcades, as the prototype of the first square in England. It was a concept that was to have wide repercussions in the next century.

After the Restoration the building in London of larger town houses was much more in line with that of country houses. This was given impetus around 1665 by the building of Clarendon House in Piccadilly. It must be emphasised that this was an unusual house, large by British standards, standing in its own grounds. In general the abiding requirement of a town house with a direct street frontage was well met by the increasing use in country areas of compact houses without wings but with lofty fronts, eminently suitable for the town. Indeed this had already been seen earlier in the artisan mannerist houses with a simple flat front slotting easily into the street scene. The compactness of the monumental pilaster-fronted houses of the Lees Court type was taken up with great vigour in Great Queen Street and at Lindsey House around 1640.

The status of the town house before 1720 is reflected in the fact that few built in the sixty years before that date were the work of considerable architects. Indeed the only exceptions were those of the group that reflected the same interests as Clarendon House, nearer to town-palaces than any other houses of the period. This group, including Clarendon House, Denham House (Piccadilly), Ashburnham House (Westminster), Berkeley House (Piccadilly), and Montagu House (Bloomsbury), stood in their own grounds and had wings, which made them unsuitable for street frontages. It is interesting that Pratt, May and Denham were all abroad at some time during the Civil War or Commonwealth, and it might therefore be suggested that this group of houses was built under the influence of what they had seen on the continent.

Brick was the most important building material for the later seventeenth and early eighteenth century house outside London, though where stone was easily available brick was

Castle Street, Bridgewater, Somerset, 1723–25. Each flat parapeted façade is joined to others to produce a uniform street

more rare. In brick sober uniformity was the product of social and financial pressures, but even the most common and simplest town-house type, that with a plain brick façade with perhaps a shell-hood over the door, could still provide an attractive street prospect, such as in Queen Anne's Gate in Westminster, Orchard Street in Bristol and Castle Street in Bridgwater. Both the Stuart and baroque types of country house influenced developments in detached town-house design, and although the baroque type is rare, there are very few towns in England that do not have an example of the typical late-seventeenth-century detached town house with a hipped roof and dormers, ultimately derived from Coleshill

Castle House, Monmouth, 1673. Tall house with a provincial nod towards post-Restoration styles

and other similar houses. Earlier they appear with the typical cross windows of the mid-seventeenth century, but latterly they become more refined with finely moulded brickwork or complexly cut and carved stonework and, between 1710 and 1730, very typically the use of segment-headed windows. It is important also to recognise that particularly in the provinces, in Yorkshire for instance, but also quite close to London, gabled houses of Jacobean aspect continued to be built well into the early eighteenth century.

Baroque houses in towns are the more interesting for their rarity. In the astylar (columnless) house-front, an order was often applied, as at The Kelton Ox, Yarm, Northumberland of c. 1670, or 29 Queen Square, Bristol of c. 1710. However, the baroque particularly used giant orders, examples of which can be seen in Marshal Wade's House in Bath and 68 The Close, Salisbury. The common baroque use of stone increased the monumentality of the houses – keystones, rustication, deeper punched windows and the use of the order all added to the plasticity of façades. In Hope House, Woodstock, and Vanbrugh House, Oxford, regional baroque variations influenced by Blenheim and activity in Oxford were evident, and these regional variations can be seen in other areas such as Somerset, Dorset and Warwickshire.

Most of the buildings considered in this book are large and their owners were determined to put on a show. The choice of building materials therefore proved a minor constraint. Most buildings, however, were built of local materials.

Timber construction was the most traditional form for smaller buildings, and although the black-and-white type began to disappear before the end of the century, timber-framing combined with brick-nogging, the practice of infilling with brick, continued. It was only really common to the south and east of the limestone belt, that swathe of oolite running from Portland Bill up through Gloucestershire and on through Warwickshire, Northamptonshire, Leicestershire and Lincolnshire to Humberside and Yorkshire, that is the overriding factor in the variation of building materials in England. In the stone areas timber-framing did occur, but although stone was the material usually reserved for grander buildings, in the limestone belt during the seventeenth century it was the accepted material even for cottages and barns. For instance, at Cirencester in Gloucestershire and Stamford in

Vanbrugh House, 20 St Michael's Street, Oxford, early eighteenth century. A startling baroque town-house perhaps influenced by baroque work in Oxford and nearby

Lincolnshire even the most modest buildings are of stone, and the same is true of other stone areas, such as Yorkshire, parts of Wales and those areas of Scotland, such as the ancient Burghs of Fife, that were prosperous in the seventeenth century. Cottages of the most modest kind have not survived in large numbers, but there is evidence of fairly widespread use of cob, and of cruck construction (a simple variety of timber-framing). Herefordshire contains the largest number of cruck-built buildings of this period; they did not appear in Lancashire or Yorkshire until after 1700.

By 1620 brick construction had appeared in almost all the counties of England except the north and south-west. Alec Clifton-Taylor has shown that further impetus, apart from fashion alone, was given to the switch from timber-framing to brick by the very common town fires prevalent from the beginning of the century. By 1700 to the south and east of the oolite belt brick was the predominant material. Elsewhere it continued to be rare except for larger buildings.

It is important to remember that, apart from farmhouses, which were of a higher status, most small rural dwellings have disappeared; most of the rural population during this period were housed in cob cottages, made of clay, or in buildings of similar ephemeral materials. Thus any survey of the vernacular at this time is likely to be, at the least, unbalanced. The traditional medieval larger house, such as Great Chalfield

Coxwell Street, Cirencester, mostly seventeenth century. Example of an unaltered street with a mixture of gabled and parapeted houses

1 and 2 Shuart Lane, St Nicholas at Wade, Kent, late seventeenth century. Pair of cottages with Dutch gables in brick

Manor in Wiltshire, had a central block containing the hall set between two wings, the three parts roofed separately. The hall began to disappear in the later sixteenth century, to be replaced with a two-storey main range, and typical of this type of house is Manor Farm at Clipsham, Leicestershire (1639). Smaller houses of the medieval tradition retained the hall centrally placed, and the whole house sheltered under a single span roof. Variations of this type included the cross-passage house with the main doors opposite and separated from the hall to form a passage, and the baffle entry house with the door in the wall adjacent to the fire-place. These were both typical lowland forms; in the south-west and Wales the medieval type of house continued to be built but with the particular regional variation of the chimney-breast external to the house prominently next to the entrance, examples of which can be seen in Devon.

The typical late-seventeenth- and early-eighteenth-century house was simpler with two ground-floor rooms, of which one

Manor Farm, Clipsham, Leicestershire, 1639. Late Jacobean house with gabled wings

Almshouses, Cheriton Fitzpaine, Devon, late seventeenth century. Thatched row with chimney-breasts next to entrances

was the larger with a central main entrance, and two rooms above. Sometimes the fireplaces would be placed back-to-back on the central wall with a central chimney stack as in the fifteenth and sixteenth century, but more often they would be placed at each end of the house, giving the very typical twin-stacked silhouette of the period. Some smaller houses of the period had the entrance in the end wall in which the single fire-place was located. The major breakthrough in later seventeenth-century design was the 'double-pile' plan that first appeared in Sir Roger Pratt's Coleshill House of the 1650s and percolated down to smaller house practice through the rest of the century. It was, of course, of particular use in designing smaller Classical houses with a centrally placed entrance in that a long mid-passage divided the two-deep rooms to either side, as at Nether Lypiatt Manor in Gloucestershire (1702–05).

Any discussion of local building types is bound to be incomplete. Vernacular architecture, by its very nature, has enormous variety, and it is not uncommon to find buildings of a type of regional construction outside their normal local area. Moreover, hybrid types are very common indeed, leading to a picture of ever greater complexity. Our perception of the towns themselves is constantly changing as more research is undertaken into the increasing commercialisation and industrialisation of the later seventeenth and eighteenth centuries. The foregoing is therefore intended only as a general introduction to a much wider subject, concentrating on the architectural side of vernacular architecture during the seventeenth century rather than on its social and economic importance.

5

THE CHURCH

The domestic architecture of the first thirty years of the seventeenth century was basically traditional, and this was even more true of ecclesiastical buildings. The characteristic style was a simple, perhaps rather vernacular, Gothic because it came naturally to the provincial masons and builders who were required to build most of the churches. As late as 1653–63 a wholly perpendicular church appeared at Staunton Harold, Leicestershire, with tower and aisles, nave and separate chancel. Although this was an exception, in that because of the sufficiency of churches passed on from before the Reformation there were few built before 1660, and certainly a very small number during the Civil War and Commonwealth, it is a late and grand example of the type to which the poet George Herbert's church at Leighton Bromswold, Cambridgeshire (1626–34), and the much more elaborate St John's in Leeds (1632–33), belong. The latter church was given highly ornate carved screens with ornament of typical Jacobean character, mostly of Flemish mannerist derivation, and this was carried over into the pew ends. The Classicism of the screen decoration was of no high order (it was in any case altered to a great extent by Norman Shaw during the last century), and this was also true of the screen of Abbey Dore in Herefordshire of 1634, attributed to John Abel, although here rather more correct and less fanciful.

Greater interest in Classicism can be seen in two very singular buildings, the Chapel of Peterhouse, Cambridge (1630), and St Katherine Creechurch in London (1628–31). Though both show some interest in Classicism on the part of their designers, it is doubtful that they were intended as fully Classical buildings, but rather as splendid settings for

St John, Leeds, West Yorkshire, 1632–33. Typical minimal perpendicular church of the early seventeenth century

St Katherine Creechurch, Leadenhall Street, London, 1628–31. Classical-Gothic hybrid style sometimes used at this time

Anglican worship. They were both built under the auspices of the Laudian church, during the period before the Commonwealth, when greater importance and magnificence was given to the Liturgy, appropriate to the dignity that the Anglican church was gaining.

Though the history of church-building in Britain before the Restoration is a little colourless, there were two impressive exceptions, and the responsibility, as with domestic architecture, was again Jones's. The Bedford estate in Covent Garden has already been mentioned for its importance in the history of the town house, but its most spectacular monument, and the only original part remaining, is the church of St Paul, built at almost exactly the same time as St Katherine Creechurch. The result, with its extraordinarily crude roof and plain Tuscan portico facing onto the Piazza, must have seemed the most alien of all Jones's buildings. The Earl of Bedford required an economical building and Jones character-

St Paul, Covent
Garden, London,
1631–33; Inigo
Jones. Jones's
Tuscan experiment

istically produced a design in which the theme of economy
became the mainspring of the architecture. Simplicity of
construction became simplicity of style, and Jones built an
extremely learned exposition of the most primitive of the
orders, the Tuscan, showing an archaeological turn of mind
uncharacteristic for the period which could have been
understood only by those of his immediate circle. It is hardly
surprising that this church was not copied at the time.

Jones had been concerned with the restoration of the near-
derelict St Paul's Cathedral since 1608, and in 1631 was
charged with restoring the Gothic east end and encasing the
nave and west end in a Classical skin. Although the completed
work, begun in 1633 and stopped in 1642, is rather strange, it
held a fascination for later architects because it dealt with the
problem of clothing the old fabric in a hierarchical way; John
Harris has shown that the simple Tuscan order was used for the
nave, and Doric for the aisles, while the transepts were in Ionic
and the great west portico in Corinthian. The portico was
especially revered and Wren projected a near-copy for the
Warrant Design he made in 1675.

Because there were few churches built after the Reformation,
owing to the fact that it took time for an Anglican liturgy to
develop and for churches to reflect that change as well as the
unsettled religious climate before the Restoration, church
building remained the exception rather than the rule; for the
invention of a type of church which combined the particular
requirements of the Anglican liturgy with the greater
awareness of Classicism, an opportunity was needed for a large
number of churches to be built. This came with the
destruction of eighty-seven churches in the Great Fire of
London of 1666. Wren's achievement in rebuilding forty-six,

plus three outside the City, was extraordinary. The sites were uneven in shape, being hemmed in with buildings, often on more than one side. The requirement was for cheap buildings which could then be adorned with fittings as each parish thought fit. Above all the feat of imagination required to design close on fifty churches without monotony was staggering and Wren met it as only a scientist could, one well-versed in the latest philosphical techniques, that of the importance of experiment in finding the ideal solution.

The most obvious new element apparent in the City churches was the liturgical layout. In response to a request for advice on the requirements of Anglican churches for the Fifty New Churches Commission of 1711, Wren wrote: 'It is enough if they [the Romanists] hear the Murmur of the Mass, and see the Elevation of the Host, but ours are to be fitted for Auditories'. This referred to a fundamental liturgical difference between the Catholic and Anglican churches, and the change, at the Reformation, away from a miraculous and exclusive Mass to a style of worship more reliant on sermons and readings from the Bible, with more purely symbolic ritual. All churches inherited by the Anglican church gave sole importance to the altar, divided from the congregation by

St James, Piccadilly, 1676–84; Sir Christopher Wren. Simple hall church with galleried aisles

Plan of St James,
Piccadilly, on
which most
eighteenth-century
churches were
based

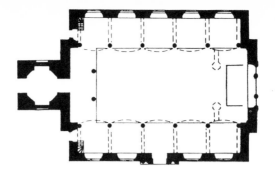

steps or screen. In Wren's churches, although the altar, now a
Communion Table, was often on a dais, the distinction of the
Communion Table from the rest of the church was neither so
marked nor intended to be the sole point of ritual interest. The
impression of light inside a Wren church was important, so
that the congregation could see, as well as hear, the three focal
points of the church: the Communion Table, the Lectern and
the Pulpit. Whereas the use of one focal point in the Roman
church led to longitudinally organised churches, the Anglican
ritual led Wren to use many versions of square and rectangular
plans.

These plans have been divided up by various writers into a
number of groups, although, because of the empirical
inventiveness that Wren brought to the task, there are a
number that do not easily fit any category. The first designs
were produced in 1670 or 1671 and include basilican
churches, with nave and aisles (St Dionis Backchurch, St
Magnus the Martyr and St Bride, Fleet Street), rectangles or
squares with one aisle (St Lawrence Jewry, St Clement,
Eastcheap, St Margaret Pattens and the later St Vedast, Foster
Lane), Greek cross within a square (St Mary-at-Hill), square
with side aisles and barrel-vaulted nave (St Mary-le-Bow),
with a dome, giving central emphasis, supported on columns
(St Antholin, Watling Street), and within a decagonal shell (St
Benet Fink). The most influential of all the types was first seen
at Christ Church, Newgate Street, and St Peter, Cornhill, both
of 1677, where the very tall pedestals support both the nave
columns and the aisle galleries, a practice that was to become
almost standard in the large town churches of the eighteenth
century. Of this type as well are two churches Wren built at
this time but which were not made necessary by the Fire, St
Andrew, Holborn (1684–92), and St James, Piccadilly
(1676–84).

Wren's smaller churches were spatially the most interesting, though the most exciting (apart from St Stephen
Walbrook), the octagonal St Antholin, Watling Street and the
decagonal St Benet Fink have both been demolished. Of those
remaining, the most exciting are those which combine the
longitudinal stress of the altar-oriented church with some
centralisation (a major preoccupation of seventeenth-
century European architects) in order to dissipate the axial
emphasis of the traditional plan and adapt it for the new
Anglican liturgy. These embryonic cross-axes were used at St
Anne and St Agnes and St Mary-at-Hill, as well as St Martin,
Ludgate Hill and St James, Garlickhythe, in the main given by
the organisation of the ceiling vaulting and the use of internal
columns to produce interior geometrical forms that cut across
those created by the exterior shells of the buildings. This
interest later became one of the most obvious features of the
churches of the 1711 Commission.

All Wren's churches have prominent altar, lectern and
pulpit, and also font, the altar with carved and painted reredos
above, usually consisting of the Ten Commandments and
Creed, written out in English for the benefit of the
congregation. The fittings of each church were provided by the
parishes themselves rather than, as with the fabric of the

St James,
Garlickhythe,
Upper Thames
Street, 1674–87;
Sir Christopher
Wren. Impressive
interior with
vestigial cross-axes

churches, from the proceeds of the Coal Tax. Wren seems to have made all the plans, which were then carried out with a degree of latitude by delegated builders and masons, although Wren's hand can be seen directly in many of them.

The most impressive of the City churches is St Stephen Walbrook (1672–77). The Grocer's Company, whose church this was, provided more money than usual and Wren took the opportunity to experiment with a longitudinal plan in combination with a dome. This dome, towards the east end of the church, is not carried on the walls, as at St Mary Abchurch

Right: St Stephen Walbrook, 1672–77; Sir Christopher Wren. The most magnificent of the City churches with domed central space

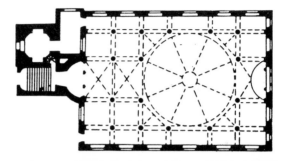

Below: Interior of St Stephen Walbrook, with a forest of columns and main dome

for instance, but on columns standing within the church, from which spring eight arches. It is an ingenious solution, but the passage from square with Latin-cross arms, shown by the semi-continuous cornice of the order, to the circle of the dome above, by the use of the eight arches, is not wholly satisfactory and remains unresolved. Still, the church is a magnificent example of the imagination of the architect, his capacity for invention and his willingness to experiment.

Invention is also the keynote of the spires which Wren designed so as to return to London its spirited skyline of before the Fire. The inspiration seems to have been the spires of recent Classical churches in Holland, under pressure from the clergy who wanted the retention of a specifically Gothic feature. The characteristic form can be seen in one of the first to be finished, that of St Mary-le-Bow (1680), the stone tower adorned with a pilastered belfry stage, above which stands a rotunda and a tempietto topped by an obelisk. The tower of St Bride, Fleet Street, has four octagons of diminishing size topped by an obelisk of similar plan. Octagonal is again the shape of the domed rotunda surmounting the tower of St Magnus the Martyr, while Christ Church, Newgate Street, has a tower of diminishing square turrets, the lowest formed by open colonnades. Certainly the most distinctive are the steeples of St Vedast, Foster Lane, a marvellous essay in the advance and recession of convex and concave forms, and the somewhat similar, though stylistically very different, Gothic spire resting on buttresses at St Dunstan-in-the-East.

Above: St Mary-le-Bow, Cheapside, 1680; Sir Christopher Wren

Wren's achievement grows when it is remembered that at the time of his greatest involvement with the City churches he was also undertaking the task of designing and later building a replacement for the medieval St Paul's, which had finally been destroyed in the Fire: so hot was the conflagration that its molten roof-lead had flowed down Ludgate Hill. Wren's first involvement with St Paul's was in May 1666 before the Fire, when he designed a new crossing with a dome for the Cathedral. After the Fire Wren, absolutely characteristically, began to experiment: initially (the First Model, 1670) with a basilican church with a domed western vestibule; then with the Greek-cross design (1672), from which developed the Great Model (1673–74), Wren's personal favourite, a wonderful exercise in the mainstream of European centralised cathedral design, with a Greek-cross plan surmounted by a dome, with a smaller dome over the large western vestibule. The last was the Warrant design of 1675, an extraordinary mix of motifs,

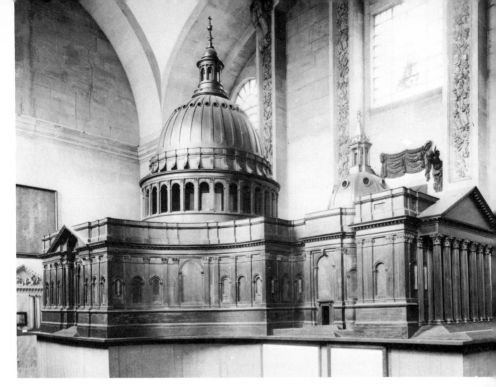

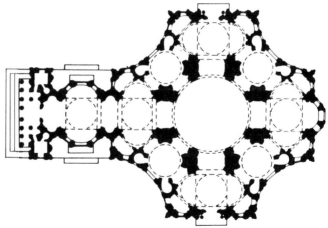

Above: Great Model for St Paul's Cathedral, 1673–74; Sir Christopher Wren. A very European scheme for a centralised cathedral

Right: Plan of Great Model

Left: St Vedast, Foster Lane, 1709–12; Sir Christopher Wren. The most baroque of Wren's City church towers

including some like the portico and the voluted transept ends from Jones's pre-Fire restoration. It seems that, although the king liked the Great Model, the clergy disapproved, and so Wren designed a traditional Latin-cross church, openly quoting from the Jones restoration, in order to get a plan approved so that building could begin – although he had no intention of keeping to that plan, as is known from the fact that the foundations laid provide, not for the Warrant design church, but for a church more like that completed. It seems that 'the King was pleas'd to allow him [Wren] the Liberty in the Prosecution of his Work, to make some Variations, rather ornamental than essential, as from Time to Time he should see proper'. A large number of the changes he did make we would consider more 'essential' than 'ornamental', but there is no doubt, firstly, that following plans accurately was not as important in the later seventeenth century as it is now, and, secondly, that Wren did not allow anybody to see what had been built while work was in progress, covering the separate parts of the Cathedral until they were finished. The most important changes he made from the Warrant design were to the aisle walls, continuing them upwards so that it appears that the Cathedral is wholly two-storeyed, which is only true of the ends of the arms of the cross and the area of the vestibules; typically for Wren these screens combined aesthetic and technological purpose in helping to dissipate the lateral thrust of the dome. In tune with his experimental method of design Wren did not fix the final design of the portico, towers or dome until necessary – it seems that early on in the building he had decided against the smaller dome of the Warrant design, because at that time he would have needed to allow for the greater weight of the larger dome in the provision of foundations.

In the broadest terms the Cathedral is based on continental precedent and the prototype of St Peter's in Rome must have been in Wren's mind. However, the exterior articulation

St Paul's Cathedral: Latin cross with large western vestibule and semi-circular transept porticos

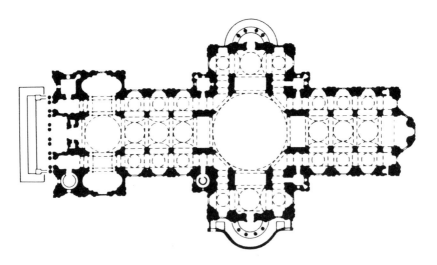

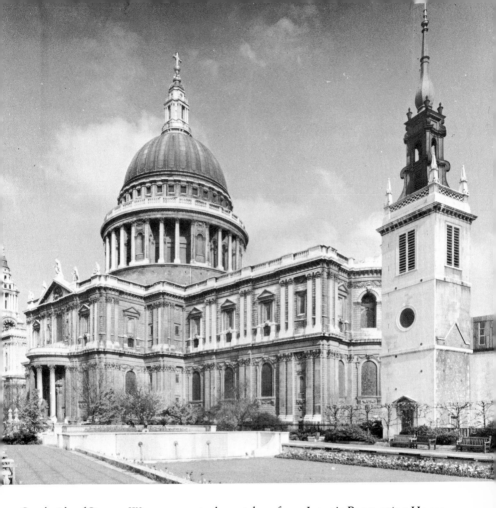

South side of St Paul's Cathedral, showing the south transept and its portico

Wren seems to have taken from Jones's Banqueting House, with the wall surface rusticated on both storeys and overlaid by a pilaster order. As the upper wall is a sham, the windows there were replaced by niches, smaller windows in the bases of these niches lighting the tribunes over the aisles. Some of the exterior motifs, for example these upper-floor niches, the ends of the transepts, the upper parts of the towers, could be termed baroque, but the main effect of the exterior, and especially the portico and the dome, is of a great Classical mind at work. The dome particularly is a work of genius, the colonnade being made to seem at rest (rather than continually spinning round, a problem with uninterrupted colonnades) by the infilling of every fourth bay. This is surmounted by an attic, the marvellous hemisphere of the dome and the gigantic lantern.

The interior is more difficult to praise because it is

St Paul's Cathedral: *Left:* West towers flanking the two-storey portico

Right: View looking east towards crossing and altar

Below right: View looking north-west over the crossing

essentially a compromise between a space with a longitudinal emphasis and one centrally planned. Earlier churches with large domed central spaces had required four massive piers to support the weight of the dome (Michelangelo's crossing piers at St Peter's are vast), but by the ingenious buttressing system and by resting the dome on eight separate points rather than four, Wren manages to make the crossing appear lighter and to increase the views around the Cathedral especially from aisles across the central space. This has its corollary, of course, in the disturbing effect of the dome not seeming to rest on anything, and it also leads to the unresolved quarters of the octagon where arches break the main cornice level of the interior and, on the level above, reveal rather unnecessary spaces behind, now emphasised by the Victorian mosaic in each. The rest of the interior is most effective, articulated by a giant Corinthian order carrying vaults with saucer-domes in both nave and aisles.

St Paul's, obviously, had little influence on church-building, but Wren's City churches were of crucial importance outside London, providing several different patterns which could easily be used for smaller churches. Some continued to be built in a simple Gothic-influenced style, Monnington-on-Wye in Hereford and Worcester (1679–80), for instance but Classicism had become relatively well-established throughout the country by 1700. Several simple churches had been built after the Restoration, probably by London architects or craftsmen, including the beautifully decorated aisled church at Ingestre in Staffordshire, possibly by Wren (1673–76), and the simpler church at Willen in Buckinghamshire by Robert Hooke (1679–80). Cross-axial emphasis was true of All Saints, Northampton (1677–80), with its seventy-foot square nave based on the same plan as Wren's St Mary-at-Hill, the two axes emphasised by barrel-vaults meeting at the central dome. The chancel was taken over from the previous building and the magnificent portico, based on that of Jones's St Paul's restoration, was added by Henry Bell in 1701.

All Saints, Oxford, probably by Henry Aldrich (1707–10)

All Saints, High Street, Oxford, 1707–10; probably by Henry Aldrich. Among the first of the baroque churches outside London and St Philip, Birmingham by Thomas Archer (1710–15) are, again, large town churches influenced by Wren, but for the first time they have more of the baroque about them. All Saints takes Wren's St Lawrence, Jewry, as its pattern, though without the side aisle, and St Philip the spacious and practical scheme of St James, Piccadilly, with galleries over the aisles. Both are externally more monumental than Wren churches, but for more complete solutions to the problems of church building in the baroque style one must turn to the work of the 1711 Commission.

When Greenwich church was blown down in a gale in November 1710 and the parishioners asked for the church to be rebuilt from the Coal Tax (which had ceased to be used for the City churches on their completion in that year), attention was drawn to the problem of providing for worship in the expanding east and west parts of the city. The question was taken up with enthusiasm by the Tories who had recently returned to power and who, as the high church party, saw the provision of the churches as an antidote to the twin evils of indigence and nonconformism, the latter then gaining ground in the poorer eastern parts of the city. Thus a Commission was established in 1711, but although it carried on until 1733 only twelve churches were built, including Greenwich and St Mary Woolnoth in the city, and towers for St Michael, Cornhill, and Westminster Abbey. The Commission, which included Wren, his son Christopher, Vanbrugh and Archer, as well as Hawksmoor, Gibbs, William Dickinson and John James as Surveyors, had a strong bias towards the baroque, and even after 1715, when official interest had begun to fade, Hawksmoor managed to keep the funds flowing both to begin the later churches and to finish as intended those already begun.

Of all the churches built under the Commission, those by Archer and Hawksmoor are the largest and most complex. Archer's, typically, show greater continental influence, particularly in the interplay between the towers and the convex walls adjoining the two main axes of St John, Smith Square (1713–28). Both this church and his other, St Paul, Deptford (1713–28), though having longitudinal interiors, have important interior cross-axes, marked on the exteriors by centrally organised side façades. Wren had been interested in combining the straightforward longitudinal plan with vestigial cross-axes, and it is not surprising to find that Hawksmoor and Archer should have inherited that interest.

St Paul, Deptford, 1712–28; Thomas Archer. *Right:* Semicircular portico under circular plan tower

Below right: Cross-axiality of the interior dampened by galleries

Left: St John, Smith Square, Westminster, 1713–28; Thomas Archer. Most continentally baroque of the New Churches

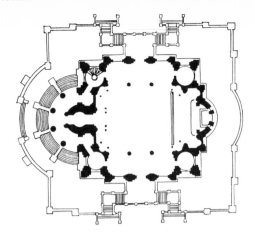

St Paul, Deptford, 1713–28; Thomas Archer. Depth of aisles plus exterior transept steps give strong cross axis

Distinct cross-axes were used in different ways. Archer's St John and Hawksmoor's St George, Bloomsbury (1716–31) are the two most striking with main entrance porticoes at right angles to the axis of the church. St Paul, Deptford, and Hawksmoor's St Alfege, Greenwich (1712–18) and Christchurch, Spitalfields (1716–31) have subsidiary side entrances, as does his St George-in-the-East (1714–29), though at each end rather than in the centre. Cross-axes are also evident in the interiors from the arrangement both of the columns internally and of the seating, and in the cases of Hawksmoor's St Mary Woolnoth (1716–27) and St George, Bloomsbury, in the central clerestories.

Typically, Hawksmoor's churches imaginatively combine ideas and motifs from antique, Gothic and Renaissance architecture and the results are parallel to Vanbrugh's houses. In many cases they are even more singular because Hawksmoor had a poetic ability in unfamiliar juxtaposition and a pragmatism learned from Wren. He reacted to the challenge of building new churches by moulding antique quotations into medieval forms. Thus the stepped pyramid of the Mausoleum of Hallicarnassus in Rome was used as a spire for St George, Bloomsbury, an octagon of Classical forms in emulation of the Boston Stump at St George-in-the-East, and corners to the nave of the same church were derived from those of the Chapel at King's College, Cambridge. As a whole, Hawksmoor's group of six churches uses detail only to underline the more powerful and emotional effects produced by the massive and often rather odd architectural forms. For instance, while the east end and sides of Christ Church, Spitalfields, are left plain, the portico is very positively

St George,
Bloomsbury,
London, 1716–31;
Nicholas
Hawksmoor.
Classical
references in
temple portico and
mausoleum spire

Christ Church,
Spitalfields,
London, 1716–31;
Nicholas
Hawksmoor.
Idiosyncratic
amalgamation of
Venetian window,
triumphal arch and
medieval spire

modelled with a giant Venetian window motif reflected in the tower above, where it becomes a triumphal arch huge enough to support an arched and buttressed pedestal on which the main spire stands. St Alfege, Greenwich is the church most clearly based on a temple, the façade at the east end, like that of St Paul, Covent Garden, blank, because the altar stands directly behind it. All the churches have extremely imposing interiors, mostly variations on Wren's ideas. The most impressive is the very Roman interior of Christ Church, basilican with cross-axial barrel-vaults over the aisles; the most complicated is that of St George, Bloomsbury, where originally the plan accounted for the shift from a south-facing portico to the east-west axis of the church (the altar was subsequently moved to its present position at the north end). The honourable exception in this group of churches is Gibbs's St Mary-le-Strand (1714–17), a simple oblong box, the portico of the entrance façade based on those on the transept ends at St Paul's, and with a simple two-storey interior reflecting the articulation of the exterior and a sumptuous plaster ceiling.

Few early Georgian churches either in London or outside can be called baroque, although some certainly have monumental exteriors and a small number vestigial cross-axial emphasis. Like the provincial baroque country houses, many

St Alfege, Greenwich, 1712–18; Nicholas Hawksmoor. Temple with cross-axis and semi-separate tower

Christ Church, Spitalfields, 1716–31; Nicholas Hawksmoor. Monumental interior redolent of Imperial Roman might

were built by architects and masons who had worked either in London or with London architects. Most of the interiors, though large and often striking, are simple, ornament usually being restricted to the chancel. Such a church is St Modwen at Burton-on-Trent, Staffordshire (1719–26), a simple stone church with a tower at the west end, using the St James, Piccadilly, scheme of internal organisation of nave with galleried aisles. More monumental are such churches as John Price's St George at Great Yarmouth, the strange exterior curves of the east end reflecting a successful attempt to produce an interior similar to that of Wren's St Clement Danes, with its rounded east end, or St Peter and St Paul at Blandford Forum in Dorset, another large church with galleries, but here the use of excellent plasterwork in the chancel reflecting its somewhat more glorified nature. The great majority of early Georgian churches, however, are simple; they derive from Wren's plans for hall churches, and they continued to be built almost throughout the eighteenth century.

Above: St George, Great Yarmouth, Norfolk, 1714–16; John Price. A large church based on Wren's St Clement Danes in London

Left: St Peter and St Paul, Blandford Forum, Dorset, 1735–39; John and William Bastard. Lavish plasterwork in a provincial chancel

One of the most important earlier eighteenth-century churches is Gibbs's St Martin-in-the-Fields (1722–26), a large galleried hall with highly ornamented vaults over the wide nave and narrower aisles. Although a baroque giant order is used on the exterior, the use of a hexastyle portico with fairly simple plain forms has been seen as an indication of Gibbs's realisation that in order to enable the church to be built he would have to adopt a style more acceptable to Palladian taste, which had rapidly taken over as the fashionable style, at least in advanced London circles. However, the Wren influence in church design in England remained paramount. Discussions of Palladianism tend to discount church design as belonging to a semi-vernacular tradition in the same way as did Georgian town-house design, but both were derived from work of the later seventeenth century.

In Scotland the standard church style continued to be Gothic well into the eighteenth century. Most churches of the period are simple, if not crude, one- or two-cell buildings, appropriate to the conservative nature of the church of

St Martin-in-the-Fields, Westminster, 1722–26; James Gibbs. The most obvious early eighteenth-century attempt at a temple church

Canongate
Church,
Edinburgh,
1688–90; James
Smith. Latin cross
church with simple
rather baroque
façade

Scotland. Classicism did not become important until the later
seventeenth century, the most impressive example being the
Canongate Church in Edinburgh, a Latin-cross basilican
church built by James Smith between 1688 and 1690. Of
course, the Reformation did come to Scotland a generation
later than England, and as there was a definite revival of
interest in Gothic decoration in house-building at the turn of
the sixteenth and seventeenth centuries, so there was in church
design. Therefore, in 1637 the Tron church steeple in Glasgow
was rebuilt in Gothic, though the Edinburgh Tron church by
John Mylne was more Classical. As the century wore on, the
Classical style gradually won equal status with the Gothic, and
one finds a church like Lauder Kirk, Borders Region, by Sir
William Bruce (1673), a cruciform church with pitched roofs
and a central octagonal lantern supporting a stumpy steeple, all
in a vernacular Gothic-Classical style. William Adam's
church at Hamilton in Strathclyde (c. 1729–32) is somewhat
similar, though it has a rustificated arched portico and very
heavy Gibbs surrounds to the windows. This church is,
however, part of a later episode in Scottish architecture, the
ingenious mixture of Palladianism and baroque that extended
into the 1750s.

6

ALMSHOUSES, HOSPITALS, SCHOOLS AND UNIVERSITIES

With the dissolution of the monasteries at the Reformation, education and care for the sick suffered a decline as they were removed from the hands of the church. In the building of almshouses and hospitals, schools and university colleges, the tradition of personal benefaction was to become increasingly important as virtually the only source for the provision of education for children and for the care of the sick and aged.

As almshouses and hospitals (in their various functions) were nearly always the work of local masons, their characteristic artisan mannerism was the normal style until the later part of the century. The Jesus Hospital in Newcastle of 1683, with Dutch gable ends to the large three-storey block which was arcaded on the ground floor towards the street, shows the tenacity of the artisan mannerist tradition in the north. The Lucas Hospital in Wokingham, Berkshire (1665), although not entirely bereft of traditional features, is more decidedly post-Restoration in style, representing the first of the Caroline country-house type hospitals, a plain red-brick two-storey building with pitched roof and short projecting wings. The Collegium Matrarum at Salisbury (1682) is the most famous example of this type, a group which also includes the Ryves Almshouses in Blandford Forum, Dorset, of 1682 and the Twitty Almshouses in Abingdon, Oxfordshire, of 1707. Most of the post-Restoration quadrangular hospitals had a similar external appearance, though larger, and behind the entrance block were, of course, courtyarded. The earliest surviving example is Bromley College in Kent, founded by John Warner, Bishop of Rochester, in 1666. It betrays its early date by certain artisan mannerist details, such as the odd size and placing of the windows, the use of buttresses and the framing of the entrance with an arch totally lacking in proportion to the building as a whole. Architecturally the most correct to be seen today, and the most impressive, is Morden College at Blackheath (1695), with the chapel in the wing opposite the entrance and the treasurer's and chaplain's lodgings in the wings of the entrance range.

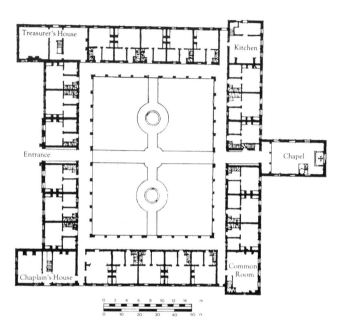

Morden College, Blackheath, Greenwich, 1695; attributed to Edward Strong. Traditional almshouse plan with entrance façade to the left

The quadrangle had a long history as a medieval building, but during the seventeenth century, with the advent of French ideas on buildings with three-sided courts closed by a screen, added impetus was given to this otherwise traditional English scheme and one sees an increase in three-range hospitals rather than quadrangles. The two largest hospitals of the period, Chelsea (1682–92) and Greenwich (begun 1696, major building completed c. 1735), both planned by Wren, are more on the scale of palaces than almshouses. Chelsea, built in emulation of and in competition with Les Invalides in Paris, the French military hospital founded by Louis XIV in 1670, is nevertheless part of the Bromley College tradition, though very much larger. Although the general building layout works well enough, the only possible criticism of the red-brick ranges being one of monotony, the incorporation of the Portland stone frontispieces into those ranges is not altogether a success

Chelsea Hospital, London, 1682–92; Sir Christopher Wren. The hospital as palace, with living quarters in the wings

Below: Greenwich Hospital, 1696 onwards; Sir Christopher Wren and others. Plan showing disposition of the main blocks

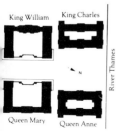

as they do not lock into the three-storey fenestration of the wings or match up materially with the brick of the wings. Wren emphasised the different character of the wings compared to the main block by giving them three storeys surmounted by an attic storey in the roof, contrasting with the tall arched first-floor windows of the main block, topped by horizontal mezzanine windows. The central range performed the usual function for this kind of building, containing the hall, chapel and administrative offices, while the wings, of a much more obviously domestic character, contained lodgings for the soldiers.

Greenwich had already been the scene of earlier building works, and it was decided that the King Charles block, the only part of the intended rebuilding of Greenwich Palace by John Webb for Charles II, should be used as the basis of the new hospital, founded by William and Mary as a hospital for seamen, the counterpart of Chelsea. Queen Mary, who seems to have been the guiding-spirit of the foundation, wanted the view from the Queen's House open down to the river, and this established the basic fact of the new hospital, that the building could have no central block, with the resulting duality of the composition owing to the lack of a unifying centrepiece. Therefore, Wren repeated the King Charles block opposite on the other side of the Queen's House axis, and formed a second court bounded by colonnades on a slightly higher level to the south, closer to the Queen's House. These colonnades masked the interior courts to the west of the Queen Mary block, and to the east of the King William block.

101

Wren tried valiantly to overcome the duality of the building in the only way open to him; he emphasised it, placing, at the northernmost point of the inner-court colonnades, domes over the entrance to the hall and chapel. Wren was responsible for siting the various blocks on the plan, and the designing of the colonnades and the exteriors of the hall and chapel. The hospital was built in a rather piecemeal fashion; the King William block was built between c. 1698 and 1704, the base block behind the colonnade probably being designed by Hawksmoor. It doesn't seem that the Queen Mary block was

Above: Greenwich Hospital, after 1696; Sir Christopher Wren. The greatest baroque ensemble in Britain, with the Queen's House in the background

Above: Allhalt's Almshouses, Goring Heath, 1724–27. Traditional almshouses with a late Dutch gable marking the Chapel

Left: King William Block, Greenwich Hospital, c. 1698–1704; Nicholas Hawksmoor. The most interesting of the base blocks at Greenwich, with typical heavy Hawksmoor wit

taken above foundation level until 1735–38 when the chapel and colonnade were built to Wren's plans to match the King William colonnade opposite; Thomas Ripley, who was then Surveyor to the Hospital, built a base block to his own, rather unexciting, design. The Queen Anne block, matching the Webb King Charles block opposite, on the river court, seems to have been begun between 1700 and 1704, but was not finished until about 1728.

Compared with Chelsea and Greenwich the remaining hospitals of the period are modest. At Great Yarmouth, the Fishermen's Hospital of 1702 is an interesting late example of artisan mannerism, though not as anachronistic as Allhalt's Almshouses at Goring Heath in Oxfordshire (1724–27). More to be expected is the simple Stuart style of the Geffrye Almshouses (now the Geffrye Museum) at Shoreditch (1710), very similar in style to the Trinity Ground at Mile End Road, London (1695–97).

Whereas almshouses and hospitals at this time presented several easily definable types, no such standardisation can be found in school buildings, and their ornamentation differs as widely. As in the development of almshouses so in schools – symmetry and the influence of Jones are not easily apparent. While such artisan mannerist schools as Peacock's in Rye, Sussex, of 1636 were built large, the majority of schools were both smaller (Peacock's School had schoolrooms on ground

Sir John Leman's School, Beccles, Suffolk, 1631. East Anglian Jacobean house with Victorian tudorised windows

and first floors) and part of the vernacular building tradition stretching back to medieval times. Most town and village schools of the period before the Restoration were of only one room but some contained accommodation for the Master, two beautiful examples of which are Lord Knyvett's School at Stanwell in Middlesex (1624) and Sir John Leman's School at Beccles in Suffolk (1631). Grammar schools were larger and though mostly Jacobean vernacular in style were, as at Shrewsbury, Shropshire (1595–1630), made up of several schoolrooms, with the more numerous masters lodged in houses nearby. Apart from rare examples, such as Peacock's School mentioned above, few pre-Restoration schools show any real Classical pretentions. Witney School in Oxfordshire (1660) demonstrates, however, that innovations in house design of such architects as Sir Roger Pratt were beginning to be seen as appropriate for school design. Externally Witney is very similar to Bromley College in Kent, retaining traces of Jacobean tradition such as tall chimneys and the traceried windows of the schoolroom. Classical references, such as the pediment over the door and porch at Read's School, Corby Glen, Lincolnshire (1668–69), were not unknown, but in the main the traditional Jacobean-vernacular school remained typical for some time after the Restoration. More prestigious schools began to be more ambitious towards the end of the century. Both the New Schoolroom at Winchester and the Upper School at Eton may have been designed by Wren; the Winchester block, small but beautifully proportioned and with crisp stone detail highlighting the restfulness of the brick walls and roof, is certainly of the quality that one would expect of Wren. The Eton schoolroom looks more like a paraphrase of the Trinity College Library at Cambridge, with its first-floor hall over a ground floor arcade, and is probably the work of a London mason conversant with the Library at Trinity and other examples of the Wren style.

Both these last buildings were additions to older schools. The importance of the years 1680 to 1720 was more in the building of new ones, often large. There was no development of new configurations, and as before the Restoration, for its external forms, the school continued to be based on contemporary house practice, meaning that most schools of the period are practically indistinguishable from domestic buildings.

The most impressive turn-of-the-century school is Sir John Moore's at Appleby Magna in Leicestershire (1693–97), designed and built by Sir William Wilson. Provincial in style, again the wings contained lodgings for master and usher. A similar plan was used for the splendid Sir William Turner's School at Kirkleatham in Yorkshire (1709). In the provincial baroque of that county with attic windows above the main cornice, it is virtually indistinguishable from a country house. The same is true of Sir John Pierrepont's School at Lucton in Hereford and Worcester (1708), although this school rather than being baroque is a late provincial example of the Stuart country house.

Bluecoat School, Westminster, 1709. A delightful example of the Baroque in little

The last group of buildings resulting from benefaction is in the university towns of Oxford and Cambridge. The later sixteenth and early seventeenth centuries had seen much building but the enthusiasm had died down by the 1630s; until the turn of the century building activity continued at a much lower level, there being nothing except perhaps Wren's Trinity College Library at Cambridge that could be compared with such masterpieces as the Schools Quadrangle and Tower of the Five Orders in the Bodleian at Oxford, earlier in the century. Worthy of note, however, is the continued use of Gothic at the universities, and though it has been argued that it was a survival reflecting the conservatism of Oxford and Cambridge, it is nevertheless true that Gothic, being the traditional style for colleges, may have been revived as the most suitable style for that type of building. This would explain the use of a totally contemporary stair-type and configuration at Christ Church College, Oxford (1640), inside a wholly perpendicular stair-well.

The first important building at the universities after the advent of Jones was the Sheldonian Theatre at Oxford by Wren (1664–69). A gift to the university from Archbishop Sheldon, it was intended as a setting for ceremonies, and Wren chose to base his design on the theatres of ancient Rome. He gave the theatre an elongated D-plan, using the curve for

Sheldonian Theatre, Oxford, 1664–69; Sir Christopher Wren. Main façade, now not often seen, extraordinarily elaborate if not actually confused

seating with galleries, but it gave him an anomalous façade to design for there were few Roman or Renaissance precedents for curved walls that did not use an order and it was imperative that the façade of two storeys surmounted by two overlapping pediments was not made to appear less monumental than it was. Therefore, the sides, curving round to the rear entrance door, were given only tall rusticated arches, but as one today sees the back of the building more often the solution was not entirely satisfactory, the façade now being close up against the Bodleian. The roof-space was intended to be used for the storage of books by the university press, and the tie-beams of the very solid roof devised by Wren can be seen in the theatre below. They appear as ropes, a part of Robert Streeter's ceiling-painting of the sky and the drawn-back canvas roof in imitation of the ancient theatre. At Cambridge Wren's uncle, the Bishop of Ely, commissioned him to build a chapel for his old college, Pembroke (1663), the street-front small but rich with four Corinthian pilasters supporting the pediment. Both the Sheldonian and the chapel at Pembroke are muddled designs; at Trinity College, Cambridge, the Library (1676–84), built after the Restoration and Wren's appointment as Surveyor of the King's Works, shows better his capacity for simple, unaffected Classicism, superbly proportioned and admirably suited to its purpose.

Trinity College Library, Cambridge, 1676–84; Sir Christopher Wren. Wren's most impressive building, Classicism at its most fluent

The long library had been the standard form for monastery and university libraries for many years past, but Wren would also have known of more recent Italian Renaissance examples, such as the Biblioteca Laurenziana by Michelangelo in Florence and the Libreria di S. Marco in Venice by Jacopo Sansovino. Although he was at first tempted by a circular plan, Wren finally settled for the long form and positioned it backing onto the river at the western end of Neville's Court. Open from the court on the ground storey, the upper colonnade separates arched windows which are repeated towards the Backs; the interior first-floor hall, a very high arcaded room with tall transverse shelves, is the most serene of Wren's creations, rightly known as the most Renaissance in spirit of his buildings. It was a simple solution to the problem of the provision of a library, and its similarity to the library at Queen's College, Oxford (1692–95), probably by Henry Aldrich, has led that to be attributed to Wren. The only other building at the universities certainly by Wren is Tom Tower, over the uncompleted gateway at Christ Church College, Oxford (1681–82). A ponderous ogee-domed octagon, it is neither survival nor revival but evidence of Wren's attitude to historical styles – a sublimation of general ideas of style that, while not Classical, is not of a Gothic that would have been known to any medieval person.

The early eighteenth century was a time of great building activity for the universities, and specially Oxford. The most important Oxford work was centred on three colleges, Christ Church, Queen's and All Souls, and included the Clarendon building to the north of the Bodleian and the Radcliffe Camera to the south. The most satisfactory reason for the high quality of the building in Oxford at this time was the presence of three capable architects: Henry Aldrich, Dean of Christ Church until his death in 1710, Dr George Clarke, Fellow of All Souls from 1680 and resident from 1714 until 1736, and William Townesend, a mason of the town. Dean Aldrich designed the Peckwater Quadrangle, a startlingly Palladian 'square' at Christ Church (1707–14), and Dr Clarke built the library that closed off the fourth side of the quad, following Aldrich's designs.

The south quadrangle of Queen's College was also begun by Dr Clarke, though with possible help in design from Townesend and Hawksmoor, and he is equally regarded as responsible for the hall and chapel block at the north end (begun 1714), based on the Chelsea Hospital plan with hall and chapel separated by a vestibule. The monumental screen

Peckwater
Quadrangle,
Christ Church,
Oxford, 1707–14;
Henry Aldrich.
The earliest
Palladian square in
Britain

Below: Library,
Christ Church,
Oxford, 1717–38;
Henry Aldrich and
Dr George Clarke

All Souls College, North Quadrangle, Oxford, 1716–35; Nicholas Hawksmoor. The most impressive example of Hawksmoor's romantic Gothic style

and gateway onto the High Street were added by Hawksmoor later (1733–36). The same courtyard scheme, based on three-wing palace plans, was used when Hawksmoor began the building of the north quadrangle at All Souls College in 1716, in an abstracted Gothic similar to Wren's Tom Tower, though with a fair admixture of Hawksmoor's individuality.

Hawksmoor's most impressive building, with a prominent position in present-day Oxford, is the Clarendon building (1712–15), built to house the university press. Although appearing to be a simple porticoed block it shows, after detailed study, the working of a complex architectural mind,

Clarendon Building, Oxford, 1712–15; Nicholas Hawksmoor. Expressive but complicated stripping back of the wall surface adding monumentality

Radcliffe Camera, Oxford, 1737–48; James Gibbs. Gibbs at his most baroque

with the use of a complicated stripping back of certain parts of the wall surface as at Easton Neston. Hawksmoor was also responsible for a number of projects for the Radcliffe Camera from the time when it was first mooted in 1712 until his death. James Gibbs, indeed, on becoming sole architect in 1736, took over the Hawksmoor principle of a round library, and built what is to all intents and purposes the last baroque building in England during the eighteenth century. The conception and detail of the dome and rotunda are particularly continental, but it seems that Gibbs was led to the use of the baroque rather than his normal personal baroque-Palladian mix because of the preponderance of the style in Oxford, and perhaps because of the continuing conservatism of the university. Although there are details with baroque overtones, that quality is manifest mostly in the general conception and its size, which was increased by its positioning in the centre of a semi-open square between the Bodleian and the church of St Mary. It is bold and exciting and one feels that had Gibbs not felt the necessity of chasing clients by offering them designs closer in style to the fashionable Palladianism, England would have profited.

Cambridge was not as important as Oxford as a centre of building activity at this time. Apart from Hawksmoor's unbuilt grand design for King's College of 1712 only two works of importance belong to this period. The Fellow's Building at King's by Gibbs, who had replaced Hawksmoor as architect to the college and whose design was based on Hawksmoor's and dated 1724–29, shows Gibbs's unwillingness to be strictly baroque or Palladian. The Senate House, however, stands useful comparison with the library at Christ Church, Oxford. Although possessing powerful baroque accents in the three-quarter columns of the attached portico and the decisive doubling of the end pilasters, the weight of the half-columned Christ Church Library is lacking in the Cambridge Senate House, where the succession of arched windows on the first floor, though weakening the composition by giving it a raised eye-brow look, lightens it also, resulting in a less monumental design.

Although the first thirty years of the century were not ones of expansion at the universities, they are of interest as a last burst before the inactivity of the rest of the century. In fact the Oxford quadrumvirate of Hawksmoor, Aldrich, Clarke and Townesend contributed to the architectural character of the town to an extent that was not to be equalled until the Oxford movement of the mid-nineteenth century began the process of neo-Gothicisation that was, again, to leave its mark on the face of the city.

Senate House, Cambridge, 1722–30; James Gibbs. Distinguished building in Gibbs's Palladian-baroque hybrid style

7

PUBLIC BUILDINGS

During the period covered by this book, town halls were not often built. Most important towns already possessed a guildhall and rebuilding only proved necessary when an earlier one burnt down or, more rarely, was considered ready to be replaced when there was money available. Most medieval market halls were free-standing and this remained the norm at least until the end of the seventeenth century. The market house at Chipping Camden, Gloucestershire (1627) has the same plan of a main room above an open ground floor as the York Butter Market (1705–06) of some eighty years later. The most familiar seventeenth-century town halls, at Abingdon, Oxfordshire (1678), and the Customs House at King's Lynn, Norfolk (1683), with a rather different purpose, follow the same traditional scheme. Larger town halls tended to be based more on domestic building. Warwick's Court House (1725–30) is a large boldly rusticated building that owes as much to monumental town-house design as to anything else. Monmouth's Town Hall, Gwent (1724), although arcaded below, is modelled very much on the lines of the West Midlands school of country house design, while the most pleasing, Thomas White's Guildhall at Worcester (1721–24), looks back to Wren and the brick houses of the reign of William and Mary.

The Scottish town hall (the tollbooth or town-house) followed a similar pattern to England, the medieval scheme of a tower-house attached to a tower for the town-bell gradually giving way to a more Classical formalisation. The Glasgow Tollbooth has long disappeared but its tower still stands, characteristically in the Scottish Renaissance style so dependent on the Netherlands for decorative motifs. The first

Customs House, King's Lynn, Norfolk, 1683; Henry Bell. Provincial town hall-type building influenced by post-Restoration style

Town Hall, Abingdon, Oxfordshire, 1670–80; Christopher Kempster. A typical town hall but with greater monumentality afforded by the giant order

Town Hall, Worcester, 1721-24; Thomas White. The William and Mary country house as town hall

truly Classical tollbooth was not built until 1703 when Sir William Bruce designed one for Stirling, a handsome building with a marvellous six-storeyed spire later copied for the Dumfries Town House by Thomas Bachop (c. 1705).

Not only churches and houses were destroyed by the Great Fire; the City Companies' Halls in the City of London also required rebuilding, and when finished formed one of the largest groups of mason-built buildings in the country, reflecting their builders' eclectic interests and partial understanding of Classicism. Unfortunately few now survive, nearly all having been rebuilt, although the College of Arms in Queen Victoria Street (1671–88) still stands, arranged around three-sides of a courtyard with plain ranges articulated by a rather Flemish-looking pilaster order. The largest municipal building in the City was the Royal Exchange by Edward Jarman (later replaced). Built after the Great Fire (1671), it combined baroque motifs such as the giant order with Flemish details in a largely untutored manner. An idea of this commercial mannerism can be gleaned from the part of the Mercer's Hall that was incorporated into the façade of the Town Hall at Swanage in Dorset towards the end of the nineteenth century.

The history of public building at this time has a curious footnote in the adoption of a very Vanbrughian style for

Above: College of Arms, Queen Victoria Street, London, 1671–88. Plain block with pilastered projections for emphasis

Left: Belvedere, Swinstead, Lincolnshire, c. 1720; Sir John Vanbrugh. Although altered, this building still has a chunky Vanbrugh feel

buildings designed in the Office of the Surveyor-General of the Ordnance. Although the Duke of Marlborough, who was reinstated as Master of the Ordnance in 1714, was a friend of Vanbrugh, there is little to show that this group of buildings originated from the pen of that architect, apart from the genuine stylistic similarity. That affinity is striking, however, and it must be remembered that Vanbrugh's style is singularly well-suited to martial themes. The military position of the country was the reason for this sudden burst of reorganisation and rebuilding in the Ordnance for, although the threat posed by the French had receded after the end of the War of the Spanish Succession, the very real threat of Jacobite rebellion had concentrated the minds of government and military most wonderfully.

The style has been singled out by Laurence Whistler and Kerry Downes as rather the Vanbrugh than the Hawksmoor Office of Works style – as Kerry Downes has written, 'round arched, castellated and big in conception'. This is proven by comparison of Ordnance buildings with others known to be the work of Vanbrugh, such as the East Gate at Blenheim, strong on military motifs, and the two Belvederes, at Claremont in Surrey and Swinstead in Lincolnshire (both c. 1720).

The Old Foundry at Woolwich (1716–17) is the least Vanbrughian of the group, being closer in style to Kempster's Abingdon Town Hall, but it is a smaller scale building (excepting the huge entrance) than the Old Board of Ordnance

South Gate, Dial Square, Woolwich, 1717. Very similar to the gates at Castle Howard by Vanbrugh

Barracks, Berwick-upon-Tweed, Northumberland, 1717–19. Vanbrugh-type motifs on a vernacular block

at Woolwich (1718–20) with its curious central feature, or the courtyarded block at Berwick-on-Tweed Barracks (after 1717), again with an oddly arched and pedimented central frontispiece, but here with heavily crow-stepped gables at each end of the block. The South Gate of Dial Square at Woolwich (1717) is even more obviously Vanbrughian, a massive banded arch topped by a proxi-pediment flanked by two machicolated buttresses. The two most extraordinary creations of the Office of Ordnance at this time were the Great Store and Gateway at Chatham Dockyard, both gigantic medievalising blocks with little decoration but the kind of emotional power one normally associates with castles. Indeed, it is strange to think that these buildings may not be the work of Vanbrugh, so redolent are they of the power of the English baroque at its most imaginative, a power that makes the baroque one of the most memorable of all English styles. Stendhal once wrote that a taste for strong emotion will always lead to the study of Michelangelo; today, in terms of architecture, it seems to lead to a study of the English baroque.

Old Board of Ordnance, Woolwich, 1718–20. The curious central feature is similar to that at Berwick

GAZETTEER

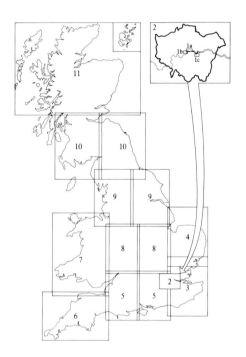

Key to symbols

⊙ town or village with various
    good buildings of the period

○ large modern town

♜ castle

✝ church

‡ cathedral

♙ house

⚅ palace or large house

⌂ town hall or government
    institution

📖 college, school or library

◙ hospital or almshouse, etc.

▲ industrial or commercial building

⌒ bridge

■ other building or monument

□ terrace, square or street

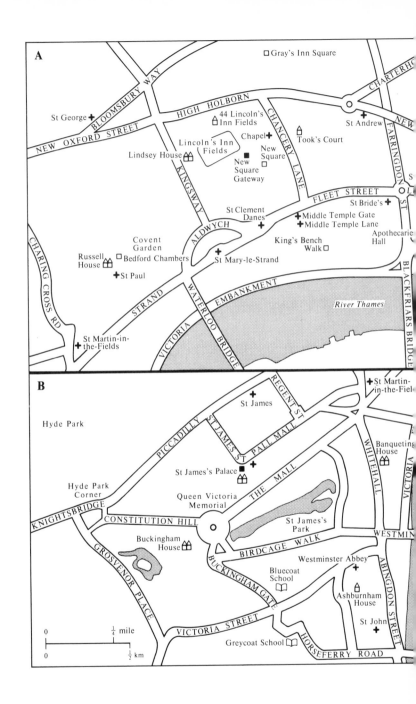

1 Central London: A – City of London. B – St James's. C – Greenwich

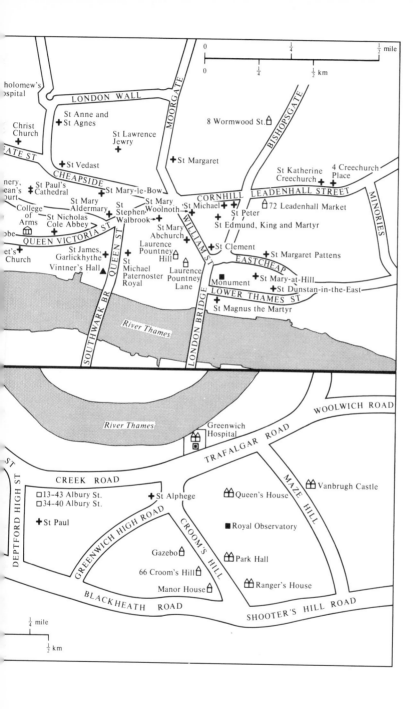

2 Greater London

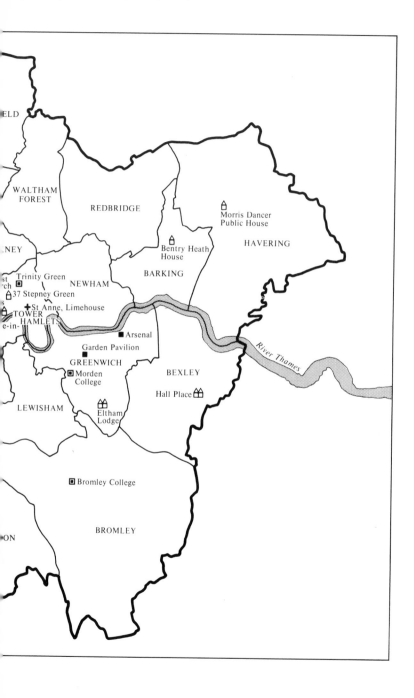

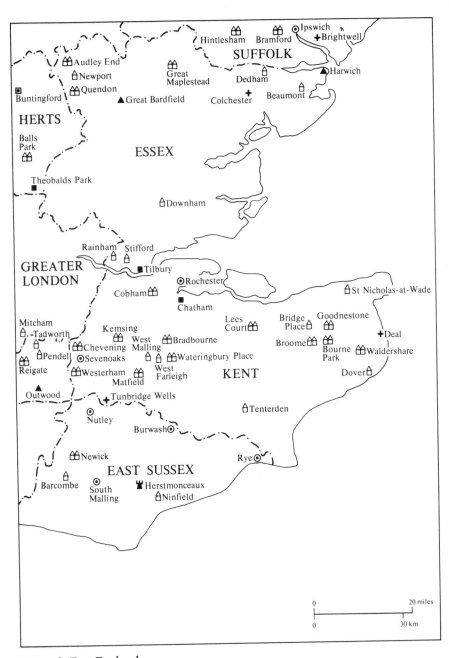

3 South-East England

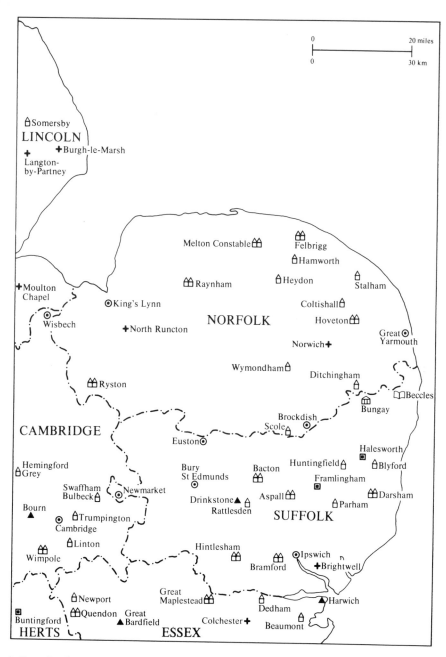

4 East Anglia

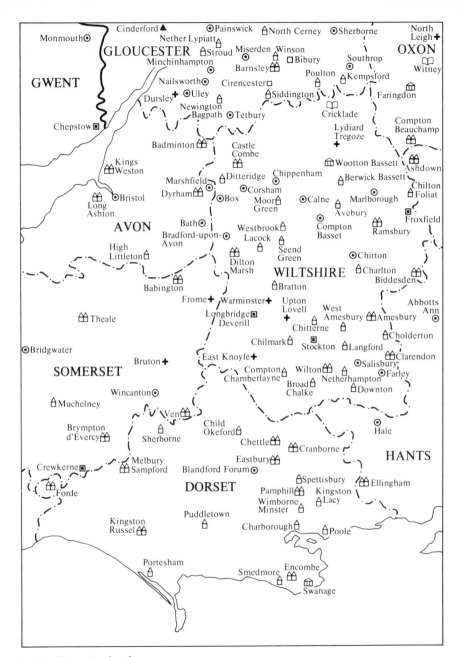

5 Southern England

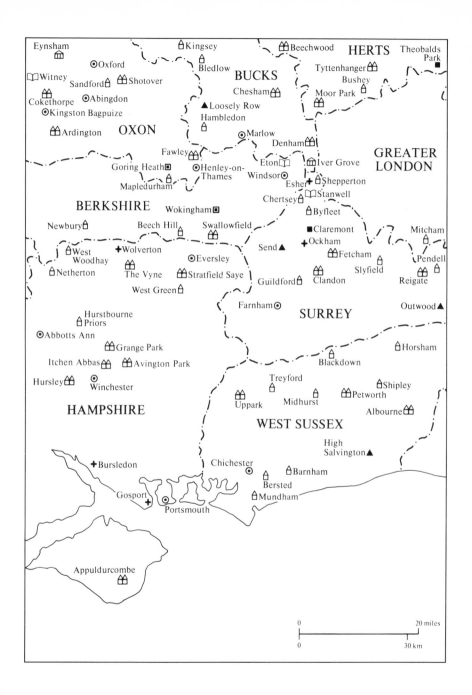

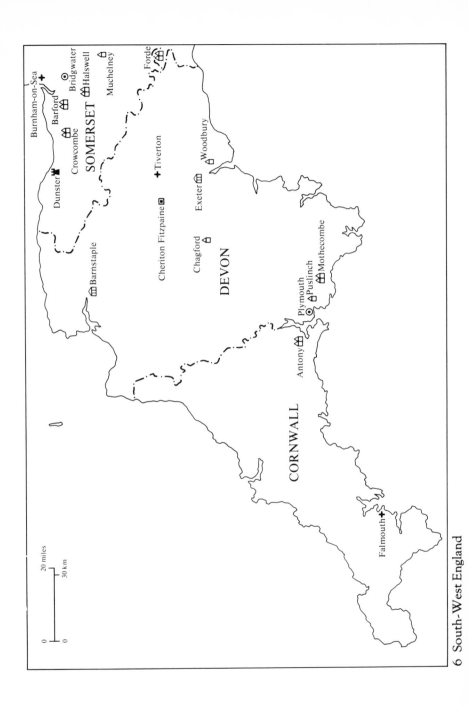

6 South-West England

7 Wales

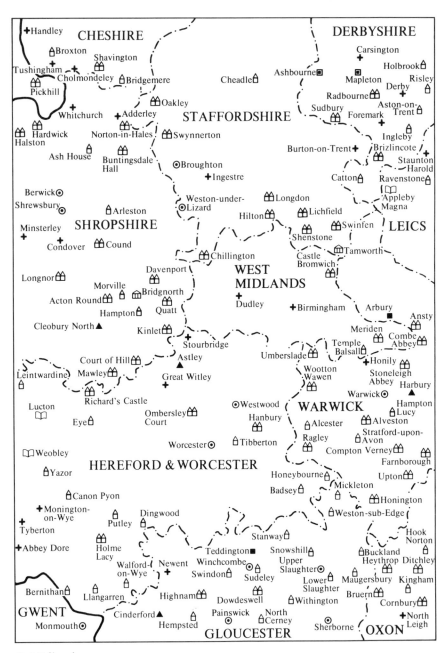

8 Midlands

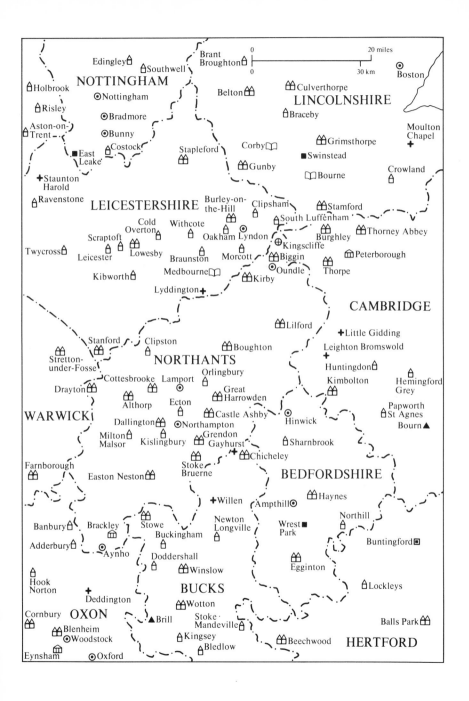

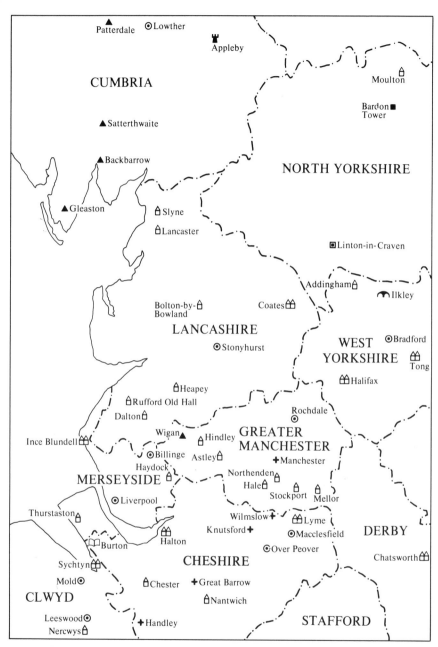

9 Northern England

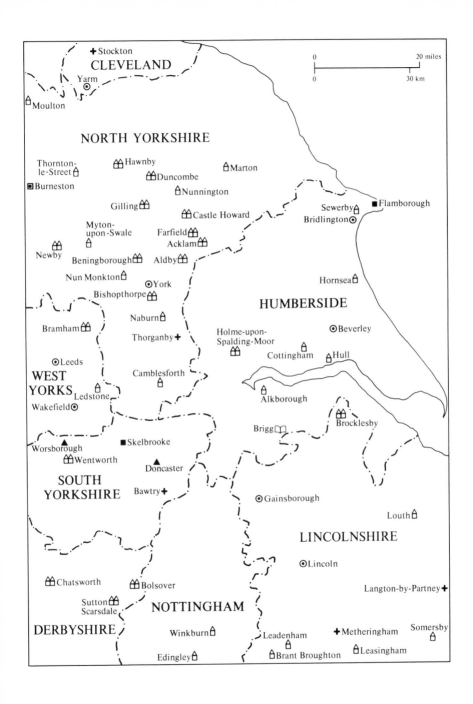

10 Border Country and Southern Scotland

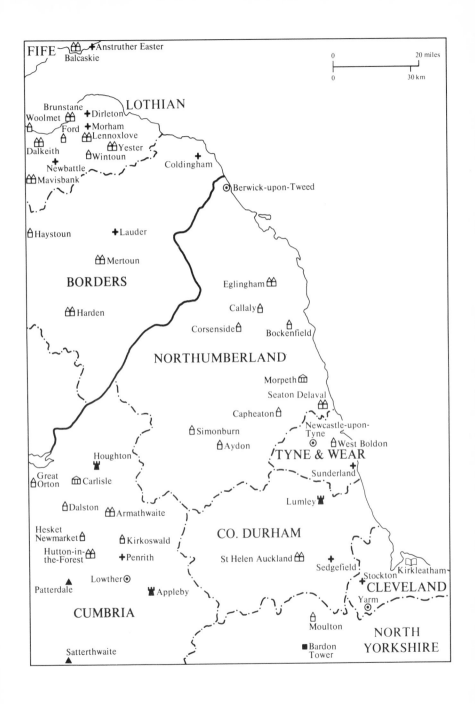

FIFE — Anstruther Easter
Balcaskie

Brunstane
Woolmet — Dirleton
Ford — Morham
Lennoxlove
Dalkeith — Yester
Wintoun
Newbattle — Coldingham
Mavisbank

LOTHIAN

Berwick-upon-Tweed

Haystoun — Lauder

Mertoun

BORDERS

Harden

Eglingham

Callaly
Corsenside — Bockenfield

NORTHUMBERLAND

Morpeth
Seaton Delaval
Capheaton
Simonburn — Newcastle-upon-Tyne
Aydon — West Boldon

Houghton

TYNE & WEAR

Sunderland

Great
Orton — Carlisle

Lumley

Dalston — Armathwaite

CO. DURHAM

Hesket
Newmarket — Kirkoswald
Hutton-in-the-Forest — Penrith
St Helen Auckland
Sedgefield
Stockton — Kirkleatham

Patterdale — Lowther
Appleby

CLEVELAND
Yarm

CUMBRIA

Moulton

NORTH
YORKSHIRE

Satterthwaite — Bardon
Tower

0   20 miles
0   30 km

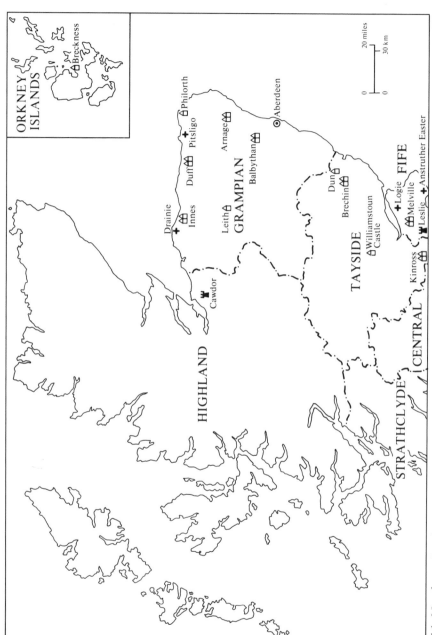

ORKNEY
ISLANDS

Breckness

20 miles
30 km

Philorth
Pitsligo
Duff
Arnage
Balbythan
Aberdeen

Drainie
Innes
Leith
GRAMPIAN

Dun
Brechin
Williamstoun
Castle
Logie FIFE
Melville
Anstruther Easter

Cawdor

HIGHLAND

TAYSIDE

Kinross
Leslie
CENTRAL

STRATHCLYDE

11 Northern Scotland

GAZETTEER

Pages of the main text bearing direct reference to the subject of each entry are indicated in brackets (italicised page numbers refer to illustrations).

Abbey-Cwm-Hir, Powys. *Tŷ-Faenor* (*140*),late C17 stone-built 3-storey manor, with centrally-placed staircase.

Abbey Dore, Hereford and Worcester. *St Mary* (75) (formerly Dore Abbey), handsome wooden screen and other fittings for Lord Scudamore, 1632–3, perhaps by John Abel.

Abbotts Ann, Hampshire. *St Mary,* 1716, typical early C18 church, small and brick with stone dressings. Coved ceiling, W gallery and box pews. *Rectory,* of chequered brick, 5 bays, 2 storeys, with hipped roof, about same date as church.

Abercorn, Lothian Region. *Church, Hope Aisle,* gallery or 'Loft' for Earl of Hopetoun, perhaps by Bruce, 1707–8. Bruce had earlier built Hopetoun House for the Earl.

Abercynrig, near Brecon, Powys. C16 house, remodelled c. 1700, with 2 short wings and steep roof. Some interiors remain.

Aberdeen,Grampian Region. *St Nicholas Church West,* James Gibbs, who supplied designs free in 1741. Rebuilding of old church was not commenced until 1751. *Mercat Cross,* by John Montgomery, 1685.

Abingdon, Oxfordshire. *Brick Alley Almshouses,* built by Samuel Westbrook, 1718–20, probably to own design, the end bay with rusticated pilasters framing arched window topped by Vanbrughian pedimented niche. *Town Hall* (113, *114,* 117), built by Christopher Kempster, 1678–80, probably to own design but with possible assistance of Wren. Tall stone block of 2 storeys with giant Corinthian order. Hipped roof with dormers, topped by balustrade and cupola. *Twitty Almshouses* (99), long low block in brick with pedimented centre, topped by simple cupola.

Acklam Hall, North Yorkshire. Much altered house (especially by W. H. Bidlake in 1912), with typical late C17 7-bay, 2-storey façade. Some good interiors remain, including staircase.

Acton Round Hall, near Much Wenlock, Shropshire. 1714, possibly by Francis Smith. Queen Anne house of 7 bays with slightly recessed centre and pitched roof. Good staircase.

Adderbury, Oxfordshire. *Rectory,* 1682, by John Bloxham of Banbury.

Adderley, Shropshire. *St Peter,* tower, 1712–3, with heavy giant Tuscan corner pilasters and obelisks as pinnacles. Rest of church 1801.

Addingham, West Yorkshire. *Lumb Beck Farm,* 1670, with back projection containing stone newel staircase.

Albourne Place, West Sussex. Fairly characteristic mid-C17 artisan mannerist house of brick with mullioned and transomed windows and giant pilasters, odd rhythm to N and S.

Alcester, Warwickshire. *Churchill House,* Henley St, 1688, brick house of 3 bays, altered.

Aldby Park, North Yorkshire. 1726, large, 3-storey brick house with 3-bay arch-windowed frontispieces on main fronts, both with well-carved pediments.

Alkborough, Humberside. *Walcot Old Hall,* artisan mannerist house of mid-C17.

Alloa, Central Region. *Church,* 1680, by Thomas Bachop, in traditional semi-vernacular Gothic. *The Old Cross,* 1690, by Bachop. *House in Kirkgate,* 1695, Classical house built by Bachop for himself.

Althorp House, Northamptonshire. Remodelled 1666–8 probably by Anthony Ellis for 2nd Earl of Sutherland. Stair placed in courtyard of earlier house, T-shaped, with galleries down both side walls. Good chapel, 1675. (Open to the public.)

Alveston House, near Stratford-upon-

Avon, Warwickshire. Chequer-brick house of Honington-type, 1689, of 7 bays, altered.

Amesbury House, Wiltshire. (28.) By John Webb for William Seymour, Marquess of Hertford, later Duke of Somerset, begun before 1660. Altered drastically 1834–40. 3-storey stone house rusticated up to attic. Heavy string-course above basement, pedimented portico, hipped and balustraded roof and cupola. Very important house for architects of later Palladian generation.

Ampthill, Bedfordshire. *Great Park House,* for Lord Ashburnham, remodelled by John Lumley, 1704–7. 11 bays wide, with 2 storeys on basement. Blue brick with red dressings, 3-bay pediment breaking into hipped roof. Enlarged and redecorated by Chambers 1769–71. *Oxford Hospital for College Servants,* founded 1697 by John Cross of Oxford. Chequered brick, 2 storeys and 3-bay wings either side of 5-bay centre carrying wooden pediment and lantern.

Anstruther Easter, Fife Region. *Church*, simple barrel-vaulted church built after 1636 with round-headed windows. Traditional broad parapeted tower with stumpy spire.

Ansty Hall, Warwickshire. 1678, brick, 7 bays with quoins. Entrance front has 3-bay centre; 5-bay centre to garden façade.

Antony House, Cornwall. Perhaps by James Gibbs, c. 1720–4. Very plain stone house of 2 storeys, with 9-bay entrance front and pedimented central 3 bays. (National Trust.)

Appleby, Cumbria. *Castle*, E and N ranges, 1686–8. East range of 6 bays and 2 storeys with mullioned and transomed windows and pilasters in 2 tiers. N range simpler, but of 3 storeys.

Appleby Magna, Leicestershire. *Sir John Moore's School* (105), 1693–7, by Sir William Wilson, loosely following plan by Wren. 3 storeys in brick with flat parapeted skyline, broken by chimneys and cupola. Schoolroom behind recessed 5-bay front, with its ground-floor arcade.

Appuldurcombe House, Isle of Wight.

Ty-Faenor, Abbey-Cwm-Hir, Powys, late seventeenth century. Manor house with chimney-stacks at the gable-ends

Built by John James for Sir Richard Worsley, c. 1701–13. 11 bays wide with 2-storey wings and 3-storey main block. Wide string-course between ground and 1st floors and continuous giant order. Pedimented wings. Now in ruins, preserved as Ancient Monument by DoE.

Arbury Hall, Warwickshire. c. 1680. *Stables,* large brick block with projecting central archway. Both Wren and Sir William Wilson possibly involved. *Chapel* with excellent plasterwork by Edward Martin.

Ardington House, Oxfordshire. 3-storey grey and red brick house, 1721, 7 bays wide with 3-bay central projection with pediment. Good interiors, including rare side-mounting 3-flight fork staircase.

Arleston House, Shropshire. Timber-framed, dated 1614 and 1630. Provincial plasterwork in drawing-room.

Armathwaite Castle, Cumbria. Front to pele tower of 1720s. Basement, 2 storeys and attic, typical of North's Vanbrughian interests at the time.

Arnage, Grampian Region. Z-plan tower house, irregular and plain, c. 1650.

Ash House, Shropshire. Early C18 brick house of 5 bays and 2 storeys with quoins and hipped roof, central bay on entrance front emphasised by pair of giant Corinthian pilasters carrying pediment.

Ashbourne, Derbyshire. *Owlfield Almshouses* and *Pegg's Almshouses,* Church St, 1640 and 1669, built of stone in diluted Jacobean style, with mullioned windows and gables.

Ashdown House, near Lambourn, Oxfordshire (33, *33.*) Built for 1st Earl of Craven, c. 1665, a hunting box high on the Berkshire Downs. Tall with balustraded roof and cupola. 2 1-storey service pavilions with hipped roofs and tall chimneys. (National Trust.)

Aspall Hall, Suffolk. Jacobean house with c. 1700 front, red brick with dark blue chequer, 11 bays, 2 storeys with a pedimented 3-bay centre.

Astley, Herford and Worcester. *Yarranton's Furnace,* excavated early blast furnace site, showing C17 configuration.

Astley, Lancashire. *Vicarage,* 1704, 5 bays with gables and windows with wooden transoms and mullions.

Aston-on-Trent, Derbyshire. *16 The Green,* 1690, brick with some diaper brickwork.

Auchans Castle, Strathclyde Region. 1644, L-plan with crow-stepped gables and corbels.

Auchindinny, Lothian Region. Small house, 1702–7, of 5 bays and 2 storeys with pitched roof and dormers built by Sir William Bruce for John Inglis.

Audley End, Essex. Alterations by Sir John Vanbrugh for Earl of Bindon, later Earl of Suffolk, 1708, including addition of screen between hall and staircase. (Owned by the DoE.)

Avebury, Wiltshire. *Trusloe Manor* house of late C17, stone with mullioned and transomed windows and hipped roof.

Avington Park, Hampshire. House with early C18 entrance front added for Robert Brydges, possibly by John James. Strange rhythm with buttress-pilasters to wings and very heavy Doric portico in central recess. (Open to the public.)

Aydon, Northumberland. *White House,* c. 1685–1700, 3-bay wide house with mullioned windows.

Aynho, Northamptonshire. *Church,* Edward Wing, retaining medieval tower, 1723–5. External appearance of country house, the sides being virtual façades, 7 bays long, with 1-bay projecting wings and a 3-bay centre, central upper window breaking upwards into pediment. *Park,* Jacobean house remodelled c. 1683 for Thomas Cartwright, S front still carrying fenestration of this work. Given further storey and pediment 1707–11, probably by Archer, and 1-storey wings. N front of 3 storeys with 5-bay centre and 3-bay wings. Stables and offices at sides of court on German model, each of 11 bays with taller 5-bay pedimented centres. Detailing typical of Archer, showing knowledge of Roman or Austrian Baroque. Remodelled by Soane 1800–5. *Grammar School,* 1671, 5 bays, still retaining Jacobean details, such as 4-centred arches to windows.

Babington, Somerset. *Babington House,* front c. 1700 of 7 bays and 2 storeys with quoins. Good plasterwork in hall and fine staircase. House altered 1790.

Backbarrow, Cumbria. *Backbarrow Furnace,* water-powered blast furnace of 1711, later much modified.

Bacton, Suffolk. *Manor House Farm,* c. 1715, of red brick with chequer of dark blue headers, 9 bays with 5-bay centre topped by 3-bay pediment. Good staircase.

Badminton House, Avon. House rebuilt before c. 1691; N and W fronts show evidence of John Webb's influence. Some Gibbons carving inside. Significantly remodelled later. (Open to the public.)

Badsey, Hereford and Worcester. *Stone House,* later C17 house with recessed centre, gables and mullioned and transomed windows, not unlike Pickwick Manor, Corsham, Wilts.

Balbythan House, Grampian Region. L-plan house, second half of C17, but with more regular fenestration.

Balcaskie House, Fife Region. (36.) Englarged and altered by Sir William Bruce for himself, c. 1668–74. Symmetrification of earlier house; some interesting interiors.

Balls Park, Hertfordshire. (17.) 1638–40 for Sir John Harrison, perhaps by Nicholas Stone. Interesting artisan mannerism with deep cornice supported by volute brackets.

Banbury, Oxfordshire. *Lincoln Chambers,* 11 Market Place, c. 1660, with overhanging upper floor, 1st and 2nd floors having oriel windows.

Barcombe, East Sussex. *Shelley's Folley,* c. 1700, brick with 5 bays, 2 storeys and hipped roof with central projection carrying pediment. 2-bay wings at back.

Bardon Tower, North Yorkshire. Tower house, earlier C16, restored and altered 1658–9 for Lady Anne Clifford. Tall, 3 storeys, now ruined.

Barford Park, Somerset. Large farmhouse, C18, to which was added high attic above cornice. Wings and blank quadrant arcades added at same time as attic. Work probably dates from 1st 40 years of C18. (Open to the public.)

Bargany House, Humberside. Brick house, c. 1675, with giant pilastered front and interesting interiors.

Barnham Court, West Sussex. Brick house, c. 1640, similar to Dutch House at Kew. 5 bays, 2½ storeys, attic with Dutch gables, other 2 storeys articulated by pilasters, Doric below, Ionic above. Garden front with 2 large gables.

Barnsley Park, Gloucestershire. (61.) Splendid rather Vanbrughian house, 1720–31, built for Henry Perrot, friend of Duke of Chandos. Little known about the house and, although it is almost certain that magnificent interior plasterwork is work of Italian stuccatori,

probably Artari and Bagutti, the suggested architects, John Price or William Townesend, were, if involved, probably working to the plans of a more capable architect. W front of 2 storeys with attic above cornice, and 3-bay centre topped by pediment. S front with 5-bay recessed centre and 1-bay wings.

Barnstaple, Devon. *Queen Anne's Walk* (formerly the Exchange), 1708. Only 1 colonnade of Tuscan columns, doubled at angles, supporting pedestal and statue of Queen Anne.

Bassenthwaite, Cumbria. *Outhwaite Hall,* 1675. Small windows, parapet and some knowledge of Classicism, such as in pediment of main doorway.

Bath, Avon. *Marshall Wade's House* (70), Abbey Churchyard, c. 1710, ground-floor as basement, the 1st and 2nd-floors with giant Corinthian pilaster order, and attic above cornice. *Rosewell House,* Kingsmead Square, a large rather florid baroque house, 1736, possibly built by John Strahan of Bristol, who may also have been responsible for similarly decorated 59, Queen Charlotte St in that city. *General Wolfe's House,* Trim St, 1707, 5 bays and 2 storeys with segmental pediments in centre of both storeys. *Widcombe Manor* (61), c. 1727, sumptuous and singular 2-storey, hipped roof house. Pedimented 3-bay centre, rusticated with giant fluted Ionic pilasters doubled and flanking it, as at ends of block.

Bawtry, South Yorkshire. *St Nicholas,* tower largely rebuilt 1712–3 in robust Gothic-survival style.

Beaumont Hall, Essex. 2-storey house, c. 1675, with gables.

Beccles, Suffolk. *Sir John Leman's School* (104, *104*) (now Leman House), 1631, remodelled 1762, windows Tudorised in C19. Leman was Alderman of London.

Beech Hill, Berkshire. *The Priory,* 1648, brick, gabled façade added to earlier house.

Beechwood Park, Hertfordshire. Stately Williamite house, c. 1702.

Belton House, Lincolnshire. (31, *31,* 32, *32.*) 1685–8, for Sir John Brownlow, attributed to William Winde. 11-bay, 2-storey, hipped roof stone house of great beauty, with fine interiors. (Open to the public.)

Beningborough Hall, North Yorkshire. (64, *64.*) 2-storey house of 11 bays with rusticated quoins and cornice with doubled brackets. Interesting use of detail, and some fine interiors, especially Entrance Hall. For John Bourchier, before 1716, possibly by William Thornton. (National Trust.)

Bernithan Court, Llangarron, Hereford and Worcester. Small detached house, c. 1695, with flared roof and late use of transomed and mullioned windows.

Bersted, West Sussex. *Rambler Cottage,* 1699, flint with stone dressings.

Berwick, Shropshire. *Almshouses,* 1672, 2 storeys with 3 ranges round courtyard and diagonal chimneys. *House,* SE façade, 1731, for Thomas Powys, perhaps by Francis Smith, of 9 bays and 2½ storeys, with ½ storey above main cornice, giant Corinthian pilasters instead of quoins.

Berwick Bassett, Wiltshire. *New Manor House,* late C17 with mullioned windows.

Berwick-upon-Tweed, Northumberland. *Barracks* (118, *118*), 1717–19, stone block with arched and pedimented frontispiece and stepped end-gables. *Holy Trinity,* John Young, 1648–52, rectangular block in stone with aisles, tripartite windows to aisles, octagonal turrets on corners of W front and clerestory windows with sub-Gothic tracery. Inside a 5-bay Tuscan arcade.

Beverley, Humberside. *The Hall,* Lairgate (now Municipal Offices), c. 1700, built for Sir James Pennyman, typical townhouse of 5 bays, 2 storeys with hipped roof and quoins. Altered inside and out c. 1780. *Market Cross,* Saturday Market, traditional type but classical with Tuscan columns, 1714. *Minster Crane,* vertical tread wheel crane rebuilt c. 1700 to replace medieval one. Positioned over the crossing, it enables 1 man to lift ¼ ton.

Bibury, Gloucestershire. *Arlington Row,* C17/18 row of weavers' cottages.

Biddesden House, Wiltshire. 1711–2 for General Webb, Hawksmoor-Vanbrugh influenced house of some quality, built of dark-blue and red chequered brick, with castellated round tower at NE corner.

Biggin Hall, Northamptonshire. Small house of late C17, now, after accretions, only visible on the garden front. Fine panelled library.

Billinge, Merseyside. *Church,* rebuilt 1718, with arched windows incorporating tracery, tower a part of W façade. *Derbyshire House,* 1716,

symmetrical house of 5 bays and 2 storeys with mullioned and transomed windows. *Fir Tree House,* Pimbo Rd, 1704, another house of same general type.

Birmingham, West Midlands. *St Philip* (89), Thomas Archer, 1710–5; tower, 1725. Large town-church of same type as Wren's St Andrew, Holborn and St James, Piccadilly, but with more baroque features, e.g. tower and doorways. Chancel redecorated internally by J. A. Chatwin, 1883–4 in style more like the Beaux Arts Classicism of interior of Madeleine in Paris (J-J-M Huvé, 1825–45).

Bishopthorpe, North Yorkshire. *Archbishop's Palace,* additions 1660–4. Rebuilding of C13 river façade by Archbishop Frewen with brick rustication, pilasters and straight gables.

Blackdown, West Sussex. *Upper Roundhurst House,* 5 bays with hipped roof and transomed and mullioned windows.

Blandford Forum, Dorset. *St Peter and St Paul* (95, *96*), 1735–9, by John and William Bastard; spire not executed, wooden cupola not to their design. Large galleried church with arched windows and pedimented ends to transepts. Inside 2 Tuscan colonnades leading up to lavishly decorated chancel. *Coupar House,* Church Lane, early C18 house with 5-bay front of purple brick in centre, red at sides. Centre bay framed by Ionic pilasters topped by pediment. *Eagle House,* White Cliff Mill St, 1730s with 5-bay E front in blue brick with red dressings and angle pilasters. *Greyhound Inn,* John and William Bastard, 1734–5, plain, 3-storey building with giant pilasters supporting central pediment. *Red Lion Inn,* John and William Bastard, 1730s, with giant pilasters and pediment. *Ryves Almshouses* (99) (Gerontocomium), 1682, of brick on U-plan.

Bledlow, Buckinghamshire. *Forty Green Farmhouse,* 1718, typical, simple, vernacular farmhouse, 5 bays and 2 storeys.

Blenheim Palace, Oxfordshire. (19, 45, *52,* 53, *53,* 54, *54,* 55, *55,* 56, 57, 117.) For Duke and Duchess of Marlborough by Vanbrugh assisted by Hawksmoor, 1705–16; completed by Hawksmoor, 1722–3. *Chapel,* left at foundation level 1716, completed by Hawksmoor 1726–31. Plain outside, pilastered inside and dominated by Kent's later monument to the Duke. *Bridge*, by Vanbrugh, unfinished in 1712, was to have been adored by towers and arcading. Now spans an arm of lake created later by Capability Brown; originally it crossed only small stream, which would have increased its formidable monumentality. *Woodstock Gate*, Hawksmoor, 1727, triumphal arch with paired Corinthian columns. (House and park open to the public.)

Blyford, Suffolk. *Little Grange*, mid-C17, plastered timber.

Bockenfield House, Northumberland. 5-bay house, c. 1680 with rusticated angle pilasters and transomed and mullioned windows, perhaps by R. Trollope.

Bolsover Castle, Derbyshire. Attributed to Samuel Marsh, c. 1670, long block with strange attached pilasters. Ruined. (DoE.)

Bolton-by-Bowland, Lancashire. *Alder House,* 1708, gabled 3-storey house with central 3-storey porch.

Bonnington, Lothian Region. *Pilrig House,* 1638, L-plan house with mannered Renaissance decoration over windows and large scrolled chimney gable over entrance of later date.

Boston, Lincolnshire. *Church House*, fine example of artisan mannerism in this area after Restoration. *Peacock and Royal Hotel*, with interiors of 1670–80. Exterior Georgian.

Boughton House, Northamptonshire. (44, *44*.) Additions to earlier house for 3rd Lord Montagu, begun 1688. 15 bays wide with rusticated ground and pilastered 1st floors, on French pattern. Central recession between deep wings arched on ground floor and, unusual at this time in England, roof was of mansard type. Architect unknown. Fine interiors decorated by Louis Chéron. (Open to the public.)

Bourn, Cambridgeshire. *Post Mill,* early post mill, possibly before 1636.

Bourne, Lincolnshire. *Free School,* 1678, attractive 1-storey building.

Bourne Park, Bishopsbourne, Kent. After 1701, 2 storeys and basement, 13 bays with centre 5 projecting with pediment, all in brick with stone dressings. Good plasterwork and staircase, c. 1700.

Box, Wiltshire. *St Thomas-a-Becket*, N aisle entrance, 1713. Tuscan with broken segmental pediment. Gothic straight-headed windows to either side, 1713.

Old School (now Springfield House), Church Lane, backward-looking early C18 block, 3 storeys high and 6 bays wide with dormers.

Braceby Manor Farm, Lincolnshire. 1653, small vernacular manor house.

Brackley, Northamptonshire. *Town Hall*, 1706, 2 storeys, hipped roof and cupola, with usual open ground floor, now closed.

Bradbourne House, Kent. Remodelling of earlier house, 1713–5. S and W fronts combining complicated articulation with intricate use of red, mauve, buff, pink and evergreen bricks.

Bradford, West Yorkshire. 634–636 *Great Horton Road,* 1697, symmetrical façade with mullioned windows. *Horton Old Hall*, Little Horton Green, c. 1670–75 for Isaac Sharpe, with gables separated by recess; hall in centre.

Bradford-upon-Avon, Wiltshire. *Bridge*, C17 rebuilding of C13 bridge. *The Chantry*, with C17 S façade, gabled, and W façade, c. 1700. *Men's Almshouses*, Frome Rd, 1700, simple 2-storey building with 4 doorways.

Bradmore, Nottinghamshire. *Rancliffe Farm*, Farmer St, *Parkyns House*, Farmer St, *Tofts Farm* and *Debdale Farm*, Loughborough Rd, and *Barn Close*. All by Sir Thomas Parkyns of Bunny (q.v.).

Bragginton Hall, Shropshire. Compact house, red brick with gables.

Bramford House, Suffolk. Beautiful house, 1693–94, red and dark-blue brick chequer façade of 7 bays and 2 storeys. Good staircase, interestingly placed in entrance hall on N European pattern.

Bramham Park, West Yorkshire. (63, *145.*) Possibly to designs of owner, Robert Benson, Lord Bingley, c. 1705–10. Interior gutted by fire, 1828, and restored by Detmar Blow, c. 1910. 11-bay block with roof-top balustrade and 2-bay projecting wings. (Open to the public.)

Brant Broughton, Lincolnshire. *The Priory*, 1658, small vernacular manor house.

Bratton House, Wiltshire. 1715, brick (now rendered), with stone dressings, very simple late Stuart façade. Rear given Regency façade, 1826.

Braunston, Leicestershire. *Chestnut Farm*, mid-C17, coursed rubble stone house.

Brechin Castle, Tayside Region. Only important house, 1695–1711, by Alexander Edward, mostly known as garden designer.

Breckness, Orkney. *Bishop's House,* 1633, small L-plan house, now ruined, with arms over doorway of Bishop Graham, last Bishop of Orkney.

Bridge Place, Kent. Built before 1639, all that remains of larger house. 5 bays by 4, 2 storeys, brick with Tuscan pilasters between windows.

Bridgemere, Cheshire. *Bridge Cottage,* timber house, late C17.

Bridgnorth, Shropshire. *Town Hall,* 1648–52, lower storey stone, now faced with brick, arched and open; upper floor timber.

Bridgwater, Somerset. *Castle Street* (69, 69), built as part of speculation by Duke of Chandos. All houses of brick, 5 bays and 3 storeys, segmentally-headed windows typical of time, 1723–5. *Glass Cone,* part of same venture by Chandos, later converted for pottery and now excavated. *The Lions,* West Quay, c. 1730, yellow and red chequer, 5 bays with basement and 2 upper storeys, half-H aprons and segment-headed windows.

Bridlington, Humberside. *Midland Bank,* Westgate, c. 1675, 8 bays and 2 storeys with wooden mullioned and transomed windows and carved eaves. Some interiors remain. *Avenue Hospital,* Westgate, 1714, 3 storeys and 5 bays.

Brigg, Humberside. *Grammar School,* 1674, by William Catlyn of Hull, fine 1-storey schoolroom.

Brightwell, Suffolk. *Church,* medieval, remodelled c. 1656. W turret resting internally on arch over pair of gigantic columns.

Brill, Buckinghamshire. *Post Mill,* possibly before 1636, owned by local Council.

Bristol, Avon. *All Saints,* Thomas Sumsion and William Paul, with George Townesend, 1712–c. 1716. Tower rusticated below with giant Tuscan pilasters with a 3-light window above, of pilasters, and segmental arch derived from St Andrew, Holborn, in London. *Bishop's House,* Clifton Green, 1711, band-rusticated central bay with pedimented doorway and 1st floor window. 2-bay wings to either side with segment-headed windows. *Bishopsworth Manor,* unusual house of c. 1725. 2 storeys and 5 bays with quoins at angles and also flanking slightly projecting central bay, which carries 1-bay pediment. Mansard undoubtedly increases impression of building strayed from environs of French or German Rococo. *Colston's Almshouses,* St Michael's Hill, 1691, round 3 sides of a quadrangle with chapel in centre of middle range. *6 King Street,* c. 1710, typical Queen Anne townhouse 6 bays wide and 3 storeys high. *Llandoger Trow,*

Bramham Park, West Yorkshire, c. 1705–10; possibly by Lord Bingley. A very plain house altered in the nineteenth and twentieth centuries

King St, most impressive of Bristol's surviving timber-framed buildings, originally 3 houses. single 2-storeyed oriel in centre, doubled at both ends, with 3 gables above. *Merchant Taylor's Almshouse*, Merchant St, 1701, of brick with quoins and mullioned and transomed windows. *Orchard Street* (69), begun 1717, all of similar type, 3 storeys with nearly even quoins. *29 Queen Sq.* (70), 1709–11, façade with 3 attached orders, at ends and flanking central bay. 5 bays and 3 storeys in brick with stone dressings and alternating pediments on ground and 1st floors over windows. A surprisingly naïve Classical house for this late date. *59 Queen Charlotte St*, 1709, refaced c. 1736, perhaps by John Strahan. 3 storeys and attic, 4 bays with pilaster strips and curiously rococo curving window surrounds. If this is by Strahan then it is probable that Rosewell House in Bath is also to his design. *Sea Mills Dock*, built by John Padmore, c. 1715, the third earliest floating dock in England, of which ruined sections survive.

Brizlincote Hall, Derbyshire. Brick house, 1707, 5 bays and 2 storeys with a hipped roof. Parapet consists on all sides of a gigantic segmental pediment across the whole façade, each containing 5 windows.

Broad Chalke, Wiltshire. *Reddish Manor*, lively little house, early C18, with 2-bay centre topped by pediment on giant pilasters.

Brockdish, Norfolk. *The Grange*, 1676, an artisan mannerist house of brick with gables and pilasters supporting a segmental pediment. *Grove Farmhouse*, 1672, much altered gabled brick house.

Brocklesby Park, Lincolnshire. Fine Queen Anne house based on the Buckingham House, London, type.

Broome Park, Kent. Early artisan mannerist house, 1635–8, on H-plan with 5-bay recessed centre. 2 storeys and attic above cornice, plus gables with a giant doubled pilaster order flanking the centre bay. 1-bay projecting wings with doubled pilasters. E and W façades equally complicated, with bays alternately wide and narrow and similar gables at roof-level. C18 interiors.

Broughton, Staffordshire. *St Peter*, 1630–4, small and Jacobean Gothic in style retaining box-pews inside. *Hall*, originally 1637, 3 storey black-and-white

house doubled in size by W S Owen, 1926–39. Good staircase.

Broxton, Cheshire. *Glegg's Hall*, earlier house given new stone façade in 1703. Recessed centre and side projections with gables.

Bruern Abbey, Oxfordshire. For the Cope family, c. 1720, with 7-bay front using keystoned windows and banded pilasters at angles, with 3 central bays projecting under pediment. Interior gutted 1780, altered C19 and 1972–3.

Brunstane House, Lothian Region. By Sir William Bruce, enlargements for Duke of Lauderdale, 1672–5.

Bruton, Somerset. *St Mary*, chancel rebuilt by Nathaniel Ireson, 1743, with Corinthian columns and pilasters carrying groin vault and delightful plasterwork.

Brympton d'Evercy, Somerset. Provincial house of 10 bays and 2 storeys with parapet balustrade and alternating segmental and triangular pediments, c. 1670–80, for Sir John Posthumous Sydenham. (Open to the public.)

Buckingham, Buckinghamshire. *Castle House*, West St, with typical townhouse façade, 1708; 2 storeys with 4-bay centre and 2-bay wings, built of brick with stone dressings.

Buckland, Gloucestershire. *Potter's Farm*, mid-C17, coursed rubble.

Bungay, Suffolk. *Buttercross*, Market Place, octagonal with Tuscan columns and arches, crowned by dome, 1689. Figure of Justice added, 1754.

Bunny, Nottinghamshire. *Hall*, 1723, extraordinary house built by Sir Thomas Parkyns for himself in eccentric style loosely related to that of Vanbrugh. Only part survives. *School* and *Almshouses*, 1700, of brick with steep roofs and dormers, all C17 in style.

Buntingford, Hertfordshire. *Bishop Seth Ward's Almshouses*, c. 1689, possibly by Robert Hooke.

Buntingsdale Hall, Sutton-upon-Tern, Shropshire. (61.) Francis Smith for Bulkeley Mackworth, completed 1721; enlarged 1857. Brick with stone dressings, with basement, 2 storeys and attic above cornice. Complex use of giant pilasters and roof-line. Some good interiors.

Burgh-le-Marsh, Lincolnshire. *St Peter and St Paul*, porch of 1702 with Dutch gable.

Burghley, Cambridgeshire. Interiors

mostly remodelled by Earl of Exeter during 1680s and 1690s, by Talman, including Chapel with good carving by Gibbons, and Marble Hall, Ballroom and State Rooms decorated by painters Laguerre, Verrio and Chéron and plasterer, Edward Martin. (Open to the public.)

Burley-on-the-Hill, Leicestershire. (46, *147*.) 1694–1705 for Earl of Nottingham. Large, sober mansion of 2 storeys with attic and basement, central pediment and side pavilions and short quadrant colonnades. Painted stair-hall by Lanscroon, 1708–12, and monumental entrance hall and saloon.

Burneston, North Yorkshire. *Robinson's Almshouses,* 2 storeys with alternating steep triangular and segmental window pediments.

Burnham-on-Sea, Somerset. *St Andrew,* with remainder of altar made in 1686 for James II and Chapel in Whitehall Palace. Altar by Wren, figures by Arnold Quellin and panels of cherubs by Gibbon.

Bursledon, Hampshire. *Chapel of Our Lady of the Rectory,* early C20 building containing a collection of German baroque fittings including reredos with twisted columns supporting a broken pediment, as well as communion rail, altar piece and assorted statues.

Burton, Cheshire. *Old School,* 1724, late example of gabled building.

Burton-on-Trent, Staffordshire. *St Modwen* (95), rebuilt by William and Richard Smith, 1719–26; completed by Francis Smith after William's death in 1724. A Wren-type church similar to that of Whitchurch, in Shropshire.

Burwash, East Sussex. *Bateman's,* 1634, fairly large gabled house with mullioned and transomed windows, nearly symmetrical, showing resilience of Tudor-Elizabethan-Jacobean tradition despite proximity to London. (National Trust.) *Rampydene,* 1699, attractive free-standing Queen Anne house, tile-hung on timber-frame typical of the area.

Bury-St Edmunds, Suffolk. *Cupola House,* The Traverse, 1693, built for wealthy apothecary Thomas Macro, of 5 bays and 3 storeys with quoins, the whole plastered and with pitched roof and cupola (odd for a townhouse). Good staircase inside. *Unitarian Chapel,* Churchgate St, 1711–2, with brick, 3-bay façade with arched windows and large segmental pediment supported by pilasters over door.

Bushey, Hertfordshire. *Bushey House,* 1664–5 for Edward Proger by William Samwell, enlarged in C18.

Byfleet, Surrey. *Manor House,* 1686, built from the materials of earlier house,

Burley-on-the-Hill, Leicestershire, 1694–1705. The post-Restoration house as palace

which may have been work of Inigo Jones. 5 bays by 2; very simple.

Callaly Castle, Northumberland. E wing (1676) of 5 bays and 3 storeys by R. Trollope. Additions (1707), very plain. (Open to the public.)

Calne, Wiltshire. *St Mary*, tower and W doorway of 1638, and interior rebuilding with Tuscan columns. *Dr Townson's Almshouses*, 1682, very simple with 4 pairs of doors on curve.

Camblesforth Hall, North Yorkshire. 7-bay house of c. 1700 and 2 storeys with hipped roof and pedimented dormer windows. Good staircase.

Cambridge, Cambridgeshire. *Christ's College, Fellow's Building*, 1640–3, of 3 storeys with dormers in roof and mullioned and transomed windows. Rusticated ground floor windows, flat-topped on the 1st floor and nearly square on 2nd floor. A good example of Italian-influenced artisan mannerism. *Clare College, East Range*, 1638–40, John Westley was the mason. 3 storeys with dormers in roof, intervals in fenestration provided by projecting bays. *South range*, 1640–2, very similar. *West range*, designed c. 1640 but not begun until 1669 by Robert Grumbold, with a giant Ionic order in a provincial Classicism. Completed 1705–15 in similar style. Very good C17 stairs. *Emmanuel College, Chapel and Gallery*, Sir Christopher Wren, 1668–73, colonnaded sides and rather baroque front to Chapel, with good plaster ceiling by John Grove, 1676. *Front Court, South range*, (Westmoreland Building), 3-storey brick building with stone dressings, faced with stone in front, centre emphasised by pair of giant Ionic pilasters carrying parapet curving up in centre to form balustrade (rather reminiscent of Chicheley House, Bucks.). *Old Court (Brick Building)*, 1633–4, 3 storeys with garrets and dormers. Gable to S, straight-headed windows, all altered later. *King's College, Fellow's Building* (112), James Gibbs, 1724–9, showing Gibb's later turn towards Palladianism. Very long block with centre emphasised by a cornice-pediment, thermal window and large aedicule to the entrance. *Little Trinity Guest House*, 16 Jesus Lane, early C18 house of red brick with ashlar dressings, 5 bays and 3 storeys with pediment over 3 central bays. *Magdalene College, Pepys Building* (1724) but seems

to be regularisation of earlier buildings, probably later C17. Pepysian Library, with bookcases of 1666, contains Pepys's Library and Diary. *Pembroke College, Chapel* (107), Wren, 1663–5, his first building, very plain externally, with a good interior including an exquisite plaster ceiling. *Hitcham Building*, E part with mullioned windows and dormers in roof. 3 west bays have dormers with pediments and large central pediments on both floors. *Peterhouse College, Chapel and Cloisters* (75), consecrated 1632. Simple rectangle built for Matthew Wren, Sir Christopher's uncle, when Master. One of the foremost monuments of the Laudian church, in a simplified Perpendicular style with a Gothic E window topped by pediment. Fine interior. Colonnades altered 1709 from depressed arches to round-headed ones. *St Catherine's College, Principal Court*, inner part 1674–87, Robert Grumbold the mason. 3 storeys with upright mullioned and transomed windows and dormers with alternating segmental and triangular pediments. Central gateway baroque, with a segmental pediment broken back, supported by giant Ionic columns over Tuscan columns on ground floor. *Chapel*, 1694–6/7, Robert Grumbold, advised by Talman. Plain, rather out-of-date exterior, wonderful fittings and panelling inside. *St John's College, Third Court*, 1669–71, brick in Italianate artisan mannerist style, with important innovation in use of double-pile plan. *Senate House* (112, *112*), James Gibbs, 1722–30, 2-storey block 9 bays wide with arched windows on 1st floor and use of giant Corinthian order of half-columns under central pediment. *Trinity College, Library* (106, 107, *107*, 108), Wren, 1676–84. *Bishop's Hostel*, 1669–71, typical post-Restoration detached house, separate from College. Brick with stone dressings, recessed centre emphasised by giant Ionic pilasters and pediment.

Canon Pyon, Hereford and Worcester. *Derndale*, small early C18 house with additions.

Capheaton Hall, Northumberland. By Robert Trollope, 1668, 5 bays and 2 storeys with mullioned windows, columned and pedimented door-surround and large pilaster-strips flanking façade and central 3 bays. Altered, especially internally, in late C18.

Cardiff, South Glamorgan. *Kennixton Farmhouse*, thatched house of 1630 altered during C18.

Cardigan, Dyfed. *St Mary*, 1702–3, nave with square mullioned windows.

Carlisle, Cumbria. *Town Hall*, 1717, 2 storeys with pedimented dormer over entrance and open ground floor. Later much altered.

Carnock Castle, Fife Region. Characteristic symmetrification of S front and remodelling of interior of earlier house, 1634.

Carsington, Derbyshire. *St Margaret*, 1648, nave and chancel, Gothic survival.

Castle Ashby, Northamptonshire. Screen to courtyard. Inigo Jones (?), rather strange low 2-storey gallery added c. 1630 to earlier house.

Castle Bromwich Hall, West Midlands. Additions to Jacobean house for Sir John and Lady Bridgeman including porch with columns after 1657 and interior alterations by Winde, 1685–1702, with plasterwork by Goudge. Wallpainting in stairwell by Laguerre, as elsewhere.

Castle Combe, Wiltshire. *Dower House*, c. 1700, with 4 gables, mullioned and transomed windows and shell-hood to doorway with volutes.

Castle Howard, North Yorkshire. (19, 45, 50, *51*, 53, 56, 57, 59, 65.) For Earl of Carlisle, 1699–1726, by Vanbrugh

Temple of the Four Winds, Castle Howard, North Yorkshire, 1725–28; Sir John Vanbrugh. More evidence of baroque interest in Palladian models, though characteristically individual

with assistance of Hawksmoor, not completed; W wing by Sir Thomas Robinson, 1753–9. *Obelisk,* 1714. *Pyramid Gate,* Vanbrugh, 1719. *Temple of the Four Winds* (*149*), Vanbrugh, 1725–8. *Pyramid,* 1728. *Mausoleum,* Hawksmoor, 1729–36. *Carrmire Gate,* c. 1730. Interior of centre block and E wing gutted by fire, 1940. (Open to the public.)

Catton Hall, Derbyshire. William Smith the Younger for Christopher Horton, 1741. Curious house of brick with stone basement.

Cawdor Castle, Highland Region. 1660–70, additions to earlier courtyard castle and keep, including central block with square-newel main stair. Entire building remodelled and restored.

Chagford, Devon. *Great Weeke Farm,* house opposite, 1696, of stone rubble, thatched.

Charborough Park, Dorset. Nothing much remaining externally, but inside good staircase of 1718, painted by Thornhill.

Charlton Manor, Wiltshire. 5 bays, mullioned and transomed windows, c. 1700.

Chatham, Kent. *Dockyard* (*118*), Great Store and Gateway, c. 1720.

Chatsworth, Derbyshire. (*18, 45, 46, 46.*) S and E fronts for 1st Duke of Devonshire, William Talman, 1687–96; N front by Thomas Archer, 1700–5; Chapel by Talman, 1687–93. Painted decoration inside house by Laguerre. *Cascade House,* Thomas Archer, 1702. (Open to the public.)

Cheadle, Staffordshire. *Hales Hall,* 1712, brick front with dormers and doorways with scrolled pediments.

Chepstow, Gwent. *Almshouses,* 1716.

Cheriton Fitzpaine, Devon. *Almshouses* (*74*), late C17, 5 cottages of cob and coursed rubble, with projecting front chimney-breasts, typical of the locality.

Chertsey, Surrey. *Curfew House,* Windsor St, early C18, with arcaded ground-floor window surrounds and Vanbrughian central frontispiece. The two houses to either side frame this one, all built as part of school.

Chesham, Buckinghamshire. *Great Hundridge Manor,* 1696, brick, 7 bays and 2 storeys with projecting wings at rear.

Chester, Cheshire. *The Bear and Billet,*

Lower Bridge St, 1664, late timber-framing, with Cheshire speciality of overhang hidden by coving. One gable, restored C19.

Chettle, Dorset. (*61.*) Attributed to Archer, an interesting house built after 1711 for George Chafin, with a very fine staircase in entrance hall on plan similar to that at Coleshill.

Chevening, Kent. Attributed to Edward Carter, c. 1630, and greatly altered in C18. Dining-room retains good mid-C17 panelling, possibly by John Webb during alterations he carried out (1655).

Chicheley House, Buckinghamshire. (*62, 62.*) Very beautiful Smith-type house built for Sir John Chester, 1720–5. Brick, 7 bays with 2 storeys and attic above main cornice. Recessed rear façade with niches in wings. S and W fronts have giant orders and cornice of W front curves upwards from sides to 3-bay centre. Good staircase and panelling on ground floor. Stables, 1723–5. (Open to the public.)

Chichester, West Sussex. *John Edes House,* West St, 1696, 3-bay centre with 2-bay wings, 2 storeys, painted cornice, hipped roof, dormers, in brick with projecting stone centre bay topped by narrow pediment. *Pallant House,* North Pallant, c. 1712 (also known as Dodo House, due to odd birds on gate-piers), brick house 7-bays wide with projecting centre, quoins and tall narrow windows. Good staircase.

Child Okeford, Dorset. *Fontmell Parva,* c. 1670, with extremely odd remodelling of 1864–9 by George Evans of Wimborne to 5-bay house with hipped roof and slightly projecting central bay.

Chillington Hall, Staffordshire. (*61.*) S front by Francis Smith, 1724, for Peter Gifford, brick with stone dressings, containing good staircase. Remodelled inside and out by Soane, 1786–9. (Open to the public.)

Chilmark Manor, Wiltshire. C17 house with mullioned windows around 3 sides of court with wall with gate-piers along fourth side.

Chilton Foliat, Wiltshire. *Vine Cottage,* c. 1700, vernacular house with hipped roof.

Chippenham, Wiltshire. *St Andrew,* Gothic upper parts of tower and spire, 1633. *34 Market Place,* 6 bays, quoins, probably Queen Anne. *Ivy House* (*61*), c. 1727. Large house with projecting wings in strange mixture of Vanbrughian motifs with something of artisan mannerism, especilly in semi-gables of wings.

Chirton, Wiltshire. *Conock Manor,* W front, with giant angle pilasters of c 1720; rest later. *Conock Old Manor,* c 1710, brick with stone quoins, with uncharacteristic basement for this type of house. Altered 1753.

Chitterne, Wiltshire. *Manor House,* L-shaped house, C17, once much larger.

Cholderton Manor House, Wiltshire. Early C18 vitrified brick house with red-brick dressing, left wing of 1732.

Cholmondeley Castle, Cheshire. *Chapel* with complete fittings surviving from 1652-5.

Cinderford, Gloucestershire. *Gun Mills,* early charcoal blast furnace, in operation by 1635, rebuilt 1682-3, rebuilt as paper mill (1743).

Cirencester, Gloucestershire. *Coxwell St* (*72*), almost unaltered since end C17, stone houses with gables and mullioned windows, all dating from end C17.

Clandon Park, Surrey. For Lord Onslow, c 1730-3, by Giacomo Leoni. Fine interiors, especially plasterwork in hall by Artari and Bagutti.

Claremont, Esher, Surrey. *Belvedere* (117), castellated tower c. 1720, and White Cottage, all that remains of Vanbrugh's house of Duke of Newcastle, 1715-20, demolished c. 1763, apart from garden. (National Trust.)

Clarendon Park, Wiltshire. House, 1737, with Hawksmoorian details, especially centrepieces of both main fronts.

Cleobury North, Shropshire. *Charlcote Furnace,* C17 blast furnace.

Clipsham, Leicestershire. *Manor Farm* (73, *73*), 1639.

Clipston, Northamptonshire. *7 Kelmarsh Rd,* late C17, cob.

Coates Hall, Lancashire. 7-bay house, c. 1700, with central pediment containing circular window.

Cobham Hall, Kent. Alterations, 1661-3, by Peter Mills. Remodelled c. 1767-70.

Cokethorpe Park, Oxfordshire. Begun 1709 for Sir Simon Harcourt. Much altered but W wing seems to be original, of 6 bays with segment-headed windows with keystones. Altered during C18 and in 1913.

Colchester, Essex. *St Mary-at-Walls,* John Price, 1713-4, rebuilt by A

Blomfield 1871-2, except for tower.

Cold Overton Hall, Leicestershire House, 1649, with definite Webb look; compare with his later houses, Amesbury or Gunnersbury. 5 bays wide and 2½ storeys high with string-courses separating storeys and strange pediment broken by arched gable.

Coldingham, Borders Region. *Church,* 1661, repaired and altered by John Mylne.

Coltishall, Norfolk. *The Old House,* c. 1715, 5 bays and 2 storeys with parapet and giant pilasters.

Combe Abbey, Warwickshire. (31.) William Winde rebuilt centre and N wings for Earl Craven, 1682-5; N wing demolished c. 1925. N saloon contains good panelling and contemporary plasterwork by Edward Goudge.

Compton Basset, Wiltshire. *Dugdale's House,* early C18 red brick house with quoins. *Manor Farmhouse,* 1699, 5-bay front with 2-storeyed porch and central chimneys.

Compton Beauchamp House, Oxfordshire. Stone entrance front, added c. 1710 to earlier house, very plain with pilaster order on rusticated basement and lower wings.

Compton Chamberlayne, Wiltshire. *Compton Park,* probably built before 1730, much altered house with drawing-room containing wood-carving in Gibbons tradition, as well as panelling and fireplace.

Compton Verney, Warwickshire. (61.) *West range,* 1714, for George Verney, Lord Willoughby de Broke, Dean of Windsor, in Vanbrughian style of Kings Weston, very plain with heavy arched windows and giant Tuscan pilasters framing the centre. Other sides altered later by Adam after 1766, and John Gibson 1855.

Condover, Shropshire. *St Mary and St Andrew,* S transept, nave and tower rebuilt 1662-79 in restrained Gothic style.

Corby, Lincolnshire. *Grammar School* (104), 1668-9, 1-storey artisan mannerist building with tall roof and 2-storey entrance.

Cornbury Park, Oxfordshire. S front by Nicholas Stone, completed 1633, 7-bay block in debased Jonesian classicism. E wing, simple pedimented block with hipped roof, 1663-8, by Hugh May. Altered 1901-6 by John Belcher.

Corsenside, Northumberland.
Dykehead, 1680, random rubble.
Corsham, Wiltshire. *Alexander House*,
early C18 house, 3 storeys with parapet
and segmentally-headed windows, rather
French. *Hungerford Almshouses and
School*, 1668, L-shaped with almshouses
in N range and strange baroque pediment
over door. W range contains inside
schoolroom with large traceried
windows. *Pickwick Manor*, fine late C17
gabled house.
Costock, Nottinghamshire. *Highfields
Farm*, 1729, by Sir Thomas Parkyns of
Bunny.
Costorphine, Lothian Region. *Dower
House*, 1660–70. Plain, T-shaped,
irregularly fenestrated house.
Cottesbrooke Hall, Northamptonshire.
(62.) Typical Smith-type house of
1703–13 for Sir John Langham, 7 bays
and 2 storeys, the corners of block
articulated by Corinthian pilasters.
Interiors later.
Cottingham, Humberside. *Southwood
Hall*, later C17, brick with 5 bays and
gabled centre projection.

Cound Hall, Shropshire. (61, *152*.) John
Prince, 1703–4, for Edward Cressett,
forerunner of great Midlands baroque
house type, 3 storeys with giant
Corinthian order and central pediment.
Court of Hill, Shropshire. Brick house,
1683, with stone dressings and hipped
roof. Some fine interiors.
Craigiehall House, Lothian Region. By
Sir William Bruce for Earl of
Annandale, c. 1695–9, moderately sized
house later altered by Sir Robert
Lorimer, 1926–7.
Cranborne Manor, Dorset. W wing by
Richard Rider for Earl of Salisbury,
1647, with low ground floor and steep,
pitched roof.
Crewkerne, Somerset. *Davis's
Almshouses*, 1707, 9 bays and 1 storey
with centre emphasised by 3-bay
pediment on Tuscan pilasters.
Cricklade, Wiltshire. *Robert Jenner's
School*, Bath Road, 1651, typical mid-
C17 school with mullioned windows.
Crowcombe Court, Somerset. (61, *61*.)
By Nathaniel Ireson for Thomas Carew,
1734. Beautiful, late example of Smith-

Cound Hall, Shropshire, 1703–04; John Prince. The earliest example of the compact
West Midlands baroque country house

type house with angle pilasters and attic above cornice. Fine interiors.

Crowland Manor, Lincolnshire. Modest, very late artisan mannerist house, 1690.

Culross, Fife Region. *Tolbooth,* 1626, simple rectangular block with crow-stepped chimney gables at each end in town famous for buildings of the period.

Culverthorpe Hall, Lincolnshire. Late C17 house, much altered C18. W front probably c. 1679, in local version of artisan mannerism. N front by William and Edward Stanton for Sir John Newton, 1704–5.

Dalkeith House, Lothian Region. (64.) Regularisation of medieval and later house by James Smith, 1702–11.

Dallington Hall, Northamptonshire. Smith-type house, built after 1720 for Sir Joseph Jekyll. 2 storeys with applied order and pitched roof above low parapet. Now Margaret Spencer Hospital.

Dalston, Cumbria. *Thrangholm,* 1683, house of red sandstone random rubble with grey dressings.

Dalton, Lancashire. *Stone Hall,* c. 1700, 3 bays, each bay flanked by rusticated giant pilasters and central bay topped by steep pediment.

Darsham House, Suffolk. 1679, 2 storeys and 10 bays with shaped gable topped by pediment. Rear of house early Georgian; good staircase.

Davenport Hall, Shropshire. Built for Henry Davenport by Francis Smith, 1726.

Deal, Kent. *St George,* Samuel Simmons, 1706; roof altered by John James, 1711–2.

Deddington, Oxfordshire. *St Peter and St Paul,* tower rebuilt after collapse (1634), completed 1683–5. Gothic.

Dedham, Essex. *Sherman's,* c. 1735, 2-storey yellow brick with heavy red dressings, rather Hawksmoorian façade framed by giant pilasters with parapet sweeping up towards centre.

Denham Place, Buckinghamshire. H-shaped brick house, 1688–1701, possibly by William Stanton, for Sir Roger Hill, with hipped roof. Good plasterwork in house, especially North Room and Drawing Room, by William Parker.

Derby, Derbyshire. All Saints, James Gibbs, 1723–5.

Dilton Marsh, Wiltshire. *Chalcot House,*

S front of late C17, brick with stone dressings, added to earlier house. (Open to the public.)

Dingwood Park, Hereford and Worcester. House of c. 1700, 5 bays and 2 storeys with hipped roof.

Dirleton, Lothian Region. *Church, Archerfield Aisle,* 1664, crudely Classical in style with Gothic window and tracery.

Ditchingham Hall, Norfolk. Brick house, 1702, with central cornice pediment. Good staircase.

Ditchley Park, Oxfordshire. By James Gibbs for the Earl of Lichfield, 1720–5, with attic above cornice, 2-bay wings and 3-bay centre. Very fine interiors including hall by William Kent, c. 1725–7, and stucco by Artari, Vassali and Serena, especially saloon ceiling. (Open to the public.)

Ditteridge, Wiltshire. *Cheyney Court,* C17 manor, gabled with rising mullioned and transomed windows at ends.

Doddershall House, Buckinghamshire. Good staircase, c. 1689, added to C16 house.

Dolgellau, Gwynedd. *Church,* 1716, provincial.

Doncaster, South Yorkshire. *Sprotborough Water Pump,* built by George Sorocold, c. 1700, for Sir Godfrey Cotley of Sprotborough supplying water to village and estate.

Donibristle, Fife Region. *Chapel,* by Alexander McGill, 1729–32.

Dover, Kent. *Maison Dieu House* (now Public Library), gabled house (1665).

Dowdeswell, Gloucestershire. *Sandywell Park,* c. 1704, wings added c. 1720, blockish house with giant Doric pilaster order and heavy window surrounds on S front.

Downham, Essex. *Fremnells,* E-plan house, gabled, using traditional medieval hall-plan, c. 1630–40.

Downton, Wiltshire. *The Moot,* lovely c. 1700 square 5-bay house, brick with stone quoins. Interior gutted 1927.

Drainie, Grampian Region. *Church,* 1666, Gothic vernacular, now ruined.

Drayton, Northamptonshire. (46.) William Talman rebuilt S front of hall facing courtyard for Sir John Germaine, 1702, and cupolas to 2 towers. Staircase decorated by Gerard Lanscroon.

Drinkstone, Suffolk. *Windmill,* 1685, one of oldest functioning post-mills in England.

Drumlanrig, Dumfries and Galloway Region. (17, 36, *36*, 37, 65.) Castle rebuilt for Duke of Queensberry, c. 1675–90, by James Smith to designs of Robert Mylne. (Open to the public.)

Dudley, West Midlands. *St Edmund*, c. 1722–4.

Duff House, Grampian Region. (65.) William Adam, 1735, for Lord Braco.

Dumfries, Dumfries and Galloway Region. *Town Hall and Steeple* (115), Thomas Bachop, 1705.

Dun House, Tayside Region. William Adam, for Lord Dun, 1730. Strange house with triumphal arch-like centre.

Duncombe Park, North Yorkshire. (62, 63, *63*.) For Thomas Duncombe, 1713, by William Wakefield. Wings by Charles Barry, 1843–6, gutted by fire and rebuilt with modifications to E front in 1890s. Terrace, one of earliest and most important C18 garden layouts.

Dunster, Somerset. *Castle*, redecoration of rooms in style of late C17, with fine plaster ceiling in Dining Room, dated 1681. Staircase with carved balustrade of Eltham Lodge-type. (National Trust.)

Dursley, Gloucestershire. *Church*, W tower, 1708–9, Gothic, by last of medieval master masons, Thomas Sumsion of Colerne, Wilts.

Dyrham Park, Avon. (46.) W wing, 2 storeys with raised terrace, 1692 by Samuel Hauduroy for William Blathwayt. Entrance front by Talman, 1700–1704, 2 storeys with attic, topped by parapet balustrade. Heavy Tuscan Orangery to S also by Talman, 1701. Stables, 1698–9, possibly by Talman. (National Trust.)

East Knoyle, Wiltshire. *St Mary*, plaster decoration in chancel showing biblical scenes, 1639, for Dr Wren, Rector of East Knoyle from 1623.

East Leake, Nottinghamshire. *Waterhouse*, 1701, by Sir Thomas Parkyns of Bunny.

Eastbury Park, Dorset. (57.) Vanbrugh, 1724, for George Doddington and nephew George Bubb Doddington; completed by Roger Morris, c. 1733–8. Demolished in 1775, except 1 wing and gateway.

Easton Neston, Northamptonshire. (48, *49*, 111, 155.) Built for Sir William Fermor, later Lord Leominster, either largely by Wren, c. 1685–9, and faced by Hawksmoor, c. 1700–2; or begun by Wren c. 1685–9, completed by

Hawksmoor before 1702. This latter argument would attribute the stables alone to Wren.

Ecton, Northamptonshire. *Rectory*, a simple Williamite house of 1693. 7 bays and 2 storeys with hipped roof.

Edinburgh, Lothian Region. *Canongate Church* (98, *98*), James Smith, 1688–90. Large transepted church with entrance façade with curved gable to nave and aisles. *Greyfriars West Church*, Alexander McGill, 1719–22. *Heriot's Hospital* (17, *34*, 35, *35*, 36), begun 1628 by William Wallace, continued after 1631 by William Aytoun and completed by John Mylne after 1643. Building shows influence of Scottish tower-houses in profile, of French architecture in plan and of Anglo-Netherlandish architecture in symmetry and decoration. *Palace of Holyroodhouse* (36, 38, *38*, 39, 41, 42), enlarged and remodelled for Charles II, 1671–9, by Sir William Bruce. *Moray House*, 1618 or 1628, irregular block but with some regularity of fenestration. Plasterwork of high quality in N and S rooms on 1st floor, comparable to that at Wintoun House. *Tron Church*, John Mylne, 1637–47, truncated 1788 and partially rebuilt 1824. Striking example of Anglo-Flemish mannerism.

Edingley, Nottinghamshire. *Manor House Farm*, 1700, typical L-plan gabled Nottinghamshire brick house of period.

Egginton House, Bedfordshire. *House*, 1696, 7 bays and 2 storeys, segment-headed windows and good staircase.

Eglingham Hall, Northumberland. Main block of 1704 added to earlier house. 7 bays with projecting wings of 1 bay each, with top parapet.

Ellingham, Hampshire. *Moyles Court*, brick house of 9 bays and 2 storeys with recessed 5-bay centre. Good staircase.

Encombe House, Dorset. Powerful house by John Pitt for himself, c. 1735, good example of independent Vanbrughianism.

Erddig, Clwyd. Brick house, 1684–7, by Thomas Webb for Joshua Edisbury, with wings added (1723). Entrance front recased in stone. (National Trust.)

Esher, Surrey. *Church, Newcastle Pew*, for Duke of Newcastle by Vanbrugh, 1723.

Eton, Buckinghamshire. *Upper School* (104, 105), Matthew Bankes, 1694, possibly with intervention of Wren.

Euston, Suffolk. *Hall*, little remaining

visible of house built for Lord Arlington between 1666–70, and enlarged by Brettingham, 1750–6. *St Genevieve*, medieval, rebuilt 1676, influenced by City churches with nave of 3 groin-vaulted bays, with similar transepts, arched windows with Gothic-like tracery and circular windows in clerestory. Very fine fittings. (Open to the public.) **Eversley,** Hampshire. *St Mary*, red and blue brick chequered church with arched windows, of 1720s and 1730s, perhaps by John James. *Warbrook*, built by James for himself in 1724, odd house with 3-bay centre, pilastered and with giant pediment containing flattened Venetian window, all topped by tall chimneys, flanked by 4-bay wings with 2-bay projecting centres.

Exeter, Devon. *Custom's House*, 1681, brick with 5 bays, 2 storeys and hipped roof. Good staircase.

Eye Manor, Hereford and Worcester. Lovely vernacular type Williamite house of 5 bays and 2 storeys, in brick with hipped roof and end chimneys. Very good stucco ceilings.

Eynsham, Oxfordshire. *Town Hall*, very small building of late C17 with hipped roof and ground floor arches, now closed in.

Falmouth, Cornwall. *King Charles the Martyr*, 1662–4, very grand internally with giant order carrying a straight entablature separating church into nave aisles. Windows Perpendicular.

Easton Neston, Northamptonshire, 1696/97–1702; Nicholas Hawksmoor. Garden façade, less sculptural than the entrance front

Farfield Hall, North Yorkshire. (63.) 1728.

Farley, Wiltshire. *Church,* c. 1690, brick, Greek cross type church with simple plaster vaults and fine entrance door. Traditionally attributed to Wren, but probably by Alexander Fort. *Almshouses,* Alexander Fort, 1682, long low building, with 2-storey, 4-bay centre.

Farnborough Hall, Warwickshire. House, 1684, with W front of 7 bays and 2 storeys, with balustraded, hipped roof and projecting middle bay. Much altered later. Good interiors.

Farnham, Surrey. *Castle,* Great Hall, refaced c. 1720, plain with segment-headed windows. *Chapel,* 1680, with excellent panelling and hanging swags of Gibbons quality. Good staircase, same date. *Ranger's House,* C17, brick of 5 bays with hipped roof. *Willmer House,* West St, c. 1720, 5 bays by 3 with giant Doric pilasters instead of quoins and with segment-headed windows. Good panelled interior and staircase.

Faringdon, Oxfordshire. *Town Hall,* late C17, in middle of Market Place standing on Tuscan columns.

Fawley Court, Henley-on-Thames, Oxfordshire. 1684-8.

Felbrigg Hall, Norfolk. Originally built 1620, but enlarged 1674-87, also 1750. 8 bays and 2 storeys, with hipped roof and dormers, by William Samwell for William Windham, and including very fine plaster ceiling in Dining Room. (National Trust.)

Fenwick, Strathclyde Region. *Church,* 1642, traditional, cruciform with galleried interior.

Fetcham Park, Surrey. For Arthur Moore by Talman, c. 1700, remodelled c. 1870.

Flamborough, Humberside. *Old Light House,* octagonal stone tower built by Sir John Clayton in 1674. Only intact coal tower in England.

Ford House, Lothian Region. Small plain L-shaped house, 1680, with ogee-capped stair-turret in angle.

Forde Abbey, Dorset. Earlier buildings remodelled by Edmund Prideaux before 1658, with very sumptuous plaster ceilings, perhaps by Richard or John Abbott, in rather heavy Jonesian style. (Open to the public.)

Fordell, Fife Region. *Chapel,* 1650, Gothic building with Classical fenestration containing Gothic tracery.

Foremark, Derbyshire. *St Saviour,* 1662, Gothic exterior with Perpendicular windows, etc. Box pews and 3-decker pulpit survive.

Framlingham, Suffolk. *Mill's Almshouses,* 1703, 20 bays long and 3 storeys in red and blue brick chequer.

Frome, Somerset. *Rook Lane Congregational Church,* Bath St, façade of 1707 with large central pediment and arched windows. Interior altered.

Froxfield, Wiltshire. *Somerset Hospital,* founded by Duchess of Somerset, 1694, enlarged 1775 with gateway and Chapel of 1813. Original half to E of gateway of brick with stone dressings.

Gainsborough, Lincolnshire. *All Saints,* 1736-44, by Francis Smith. *Friends Meeting House,* 1704-5.

Gayhurst, Buckinghamshire. *Church,* 1728, small beautiful church, pedimented box with chancel and tower, pilastered interior. High quality plasterwork inside.

Gilling Castle, North Yorkshire. (63.) Probably built by William Wakefield, for 8th and 9th Viscounts Fairfax, c. 1719-38. Fine interiors.

Glasgow, Strathclyde Region. *Merchant's Hall,* steeple by Sir William Bruce (?), 1651-9, Wren-like, 4-storied steeple in mixture of Classical and Gothic.

Gleaston, Cumbria. *Corn Mills,* two watermills, both probably C17.

Goodnestone Park, Kent. Simple house of purple brick with red dressings, 3 storeys with projecting pedimented centre. Altered late C18.

Goring Heath, Oxfordshire. *Almshouses* (103, *103*) founded by Henry Allhalt, Lord Mayor of London, 1724. 1 storey round 3 sides of courtyard, chapel in centre block. Some good original fittings.

Gosport, Hampshire. *Holy Trinity,* probably based on King Charles the Martyr in Falmouth, church of 1696 given strange Victorian exterior by Arthur Blomfield in 1887.

Grange Park, Hampshire. Built by William Samwell for Sir Robert Henley, c. 1670; remodelled by Wilkins, 1809, and Cockerell, 1823-5; now existing only as shell, the C17 work unrecognisable. (Owned by the DoE.)

Granton, Lothian Region. *Caroline Park,* 1685, late courtyard house with strange S front (1696) with heavy rustication and bowed roofs. N front regular with 2 chimney gables and balustrade on

cornice, but with irregular fenestration.
Great Bardfield, Essex. *Gibraltar Mill,*
built as smock mill in 1680 and
successively converted into cottage in
early C18 and heightened to become
tower mill (1760), finally to be
reconverted back into house.
Great Barrow, Cheshire. *Church,*
chancel, 1671, in Gothic with mullioned
windows with arched lights.
Great Harrowden, Northamptonshire.
Harrowden Hall, c. 1694.
Great Maplestead, Essex. *Dynes Hall,*
1689, hipped roof, Williamite house of
red and blue brick chequer.
Great Orton, Cumbria. *House* of
c. 1700, cruck with clay walls on stone
plinth.
Great Witley, Hereford and Worcester.
St Michael, consecrated 1735, but using
parts of Duke of Chandos's chapel at
Cannons (1713–20), demolished in
1747, including ceiling-paintings (by
Antonio Bellucci), copies of stucco (by
Bagutti) and painted glass (Francisco
Sleter).
Great Yarmouth, Norfolk. *St George*
(95, *96*), John Price assisted by son John,
1714–6. *20 South Quay* (now Custom's
House), 1720, brick with stone dressings
and segment-headed windows.
Fishermen's Hospital, 1702, artisan
mannerist brick, 3 wings.
Grendon Hall, Northamptonshire.
Now Northants County Youth Centre,
plain early C18 house of Honington-type,
N side rather older (probably mid-C17).
Grimsthorpe Castle, Lincolnshire. (57,
58, *58*.) N front rebuilt for Duke of
Ancaster, 1722–6, by Vanbrugh. S front
projected but not built. Vanbrugh was
also responsible for central hall and
flanking staircases.
Guildford, Surrey. *Guildford House,*
155, High St, 1660, with bays separated
on upper floors by pilasters and with
carved foliage under ground-floor
windows.
Gunby Hall, Lincolnshire. 1700, brick
with stone dressings, characteristic
Queen Anne house with centre of garden
front recessed.
Hale, Hampshire. *Church,* Thomas
Archer, 1717, at own expense rebuilt
nave and added chancel. *House,* after
1715, by Thomas Archer for himself.
Hale Manor House, Greater
Manchester. Brick house with stone
dressings, c. 1700.

Halesworth, Suffolk. *Almshouses,* 1686,
brick with odd gable ends.
Halifax, West Yorkshire. *Scout Hall,*
large, oddly fenestrated house of
1694(?).
Halston Hall, Shropshire. Brick house,
1690, 2 storeys with projecting centre.
Halswell House, Somerset. 1689,
added to earlier house, plain with
interesting central doorway and 1st floor
window aedicule.
Halton, Cheshire. *House* of brick,
c. 1710, with monumental stables,
articulated by giant pilasters.
Hambledon, Buckinghamshire. *Rectory,*
brick, 1724.
Hamilton, Strathclyde Region. *Church*
(98), William Adam, c. 1729–32,
circular with Greek cross arm.
Hampton Hall, Shropshire. Red brick
house, c. 1680–5.
Hampton Lucy, Warwickshire. *Rectory,*
perhaps by Francis Smith, 1721.
Hamworth Hall, Norfolk. Early C18
brick house with hipped roof.
Hanbury Hall, Hereford and
Worcester. (31.) For Thomas Vernon,
1701, built by William Rudhall. 11 bays
and 2 storeys with a 5-bay central
recession, hipped roof and dormers. The
central 3-bay cornice pediment is, oddly,
supported on a pair of Corinthian
columns. The interior is very fine with
painted ceiling to hall, and walls and
ceiling of square-newel staircase painted
by Thornhill (1710 or soon after).
(National Trust.)
Handley, Cheshire. *Church,* excellent
hammerbeam roof of 1662 with fine
corbels.
Harbury, Warwickshire. *Chesterton
Windmill,* 1632, for Sir Edward Peyto,
either by Peyto or by Nicholas Stone. A
magnificent stone mill standing on 6
arches, base probably built for another
purpose originally.
Harden House, Borders Region. Large
basemented house, 1703–c. 1707.
Hardwick Hall, Shropshire. Brick
house, c. 1720 with wings of Smith type
with giant pilasters.
Harwich, Essex. *Shipyard Crane,*
installed 1667 in Harwich Navy Yard,
moved 1928.
Hawnby, North Yorkshire. *Arden Hall,*
stone house of early C18 with 3rd storey
added later.
Haydock, Merseyside. *Woodhouse Farm,*
early C18, brick with stone quoins.

Haynes, Bedfordshire. *Hawnes Park* (62), built for Lord Cartaret by Thomas Ripley, c. 1720. Very long W front with centre and ends marked by pilasters. E front remodelled by Cubitt, 1849–50; also altered 1790 by James Lewis.

Haystoun House, Borders Region. 1660, simple, low, vernacular L-shaped house.

Heapey, Lancashire. *Cliff Farm*, 1696, coursed rubble.

Hemingford Grey House, Cambridgeshire. Red brick house, 1697, with segment-headed windows and hipped roof.

Hempsted House, Gloucestershire. 1671, brick house with late Jacobean-artisan mannerist detail.

Henley-on-Thames, Oxfordshire. *Longlands*, Hart St, c. 1720, red and yellow brick house with angle-pilasters and segment-headed windows. *Nettlebed Brick Kiln*, most unusual tapering kiln, probably C17.

Herstmonceaux Castle, East Sussex. Good staircase of c. 1675, of Eltham Lodge type with carved floral panels, from Wheatley Hall, Doncaster.

Hesket Newmarket, Cumbria. *House*, C17, stone.

Heydon, Norfolk. *Cropton Hall*, 5-bay and 2-storey house, c. 1700, with large gable.

Heythrop, Oxfordshire. (19, 45, 47.) Designed by Archer and built by Francis Smith, c. 1707–10. No interiors; gutted by fire 1831. Present interiors by Alfred Waterhouse, 1871.

High Littleton, Avon. Interesting house, c. 1710, 2½ storeys with mullioned and transomed windows on 2nd floor, segmentally-headed windows below.

High Salvington, West Sussex. *Windmill*, well-preserved post-mill, c. 1700.

Highnam Court, Gloucestershire. 2-storey house of brick with stone dressings, of Thorpe Hall type of artisan mannerism. Good mid-C18 plasterwork inside by William Stocking; altered c. 1840 by Lewis Vulliamy, and again in the 1870s.

Hilton Park, Staffordshire. Smith type house of early C18, 2 storeys, and attic above cornice added during C19.

Hindley, Greater Manchester. *Laurel House*, Atherton Rd, 1714, 5 bays with sash windows.

Hintlesham Hall, Suffolk. Elizabethan house remodelled c. 1720. Ground floor rusticated below 1st floor with Corinthian pilaster order with central Venetian window. Wings, parapet pediment. Fine stucco ceiling in Drawing Room, c. 1690.

Hinwick, Bedfordshire. *Hall*, earlier house given new orientation and motifs, similar to Hinwick House, early in C18, by General Livesay. *House*, 1709–14, for Richard Orlebar, 2 storeys, attic above cornice. 3-bay centre to E wing framed by pilasters, which also mark corners of block. Niches beside central bay of S end which is topped by very tall pediment in attic.

Holbrook Hall, Derbyshire. 1681, typical post-Restoration house, 5 bays and 2 storeys of stone with quoins.

Holme Lacy, Hereford and Worcester. (31.) 1673 and afterwards, probably by Hugh May, for 1st Viscount Scudamore. Very fine interiors, especially 9 plaster ceilings.

Holme-upon-Spalding-Moor, Humberside. *Holme Hall*, c. 1720–23 to designs by William Wakefield for Lord Langdale, later enlarged. Plain 9-bay front; good staircase.

Honeybourne, Hereford and Worcester. *The Gables*, late C17, coursed rubble.

Honily, Warwickshire. *Church*, 1723.

Honington Hall, Warwickshire. Very beautiful house built for Sir Henry Parker, 1682. 7-bay wide entrance front with recessed 3-bay centre, brick and stone dressings, hipped roof and dormers. Oval recesses with busts of emperors in spaces between upper and lower windows. Alterations to S and garden front, and to interior, c. 1740–50.

Hook Norton, Oxfordshire. *Lodge Farm*, 1646, L-plan, random rubble.

Hopetoun House, Lothian Region. (39, 39, 64, 65, 65.) 1699–1703, Sir William Bruce for Charles Hope, later 1st Earl of Hopetoun, now only recognisable from garden side. Enlarged and remodelled by William, John and Robert Adam, 1723–56.

Hornsea, Humberside. *Old Hall*, brick house, mid-C17, with shaped gables and projecting wings to front.

Horsham, West Sussex. *Horsham Park* (now Council Offices), c. 1720, with central pediment and segment-headed windows. Garden side c. 1740.

Houghton, Cumbria. *Drawdykes Castle,* addition to peletower (1676), provincial Classicism with windows with alternating triangular and segmental pediments.

Hoveton House, Norfolk. Brick house with hipped roof and dormers, c. 1700, 3 middle bays projecting and flanked by giant pilasters carrying steep pediment.

Hull, Humberside. *Wilberforce House,* High Street, brick town house, c. 1660, with 3-storey frontispiece 1 bay wide, 1st and 2nd floors framed by pair of giant pilasters. 1 panelled room inside, remainder remodelled c. 1750.

Huntingdon, Cambridgeshire. *Walden House,* Market Hill, late C17 house of red brick framed by giant pilasters and with garlands below 1st floor window.

Huntingfield, Suffolk. *High House,* 1700, compact house with rounded end gables and smaller side gables.

Hursley Park, Hampshire. (62.) 11-bay house, c. 1720, of 2 storeys with basement, fronted by portico of 4 giant Doric pilasters. Extended during early C20 by A Marshall Mackenzie.

Hurstbourne Priors, Hampshire. Andover Lodge, early C18, Grey and red brick tower made up of arched recesses and windows, all rather Vanbrughian. Possibly by Archer who designed a house for the site (1712).

Hutton-in-the Forest, Cumbria. *House,* 1685, with front centrepiece of 3 storeys and 5 bays with parapet and mullioned and transomed windows; the wider central bay has larger window with flanking pilasters and balcony on 1st floor.

Ilkley, West Yorkshire. *Bridge,* probably 1673, later repaired.

Ince Blundell Hall, Merseyside. Garden façade of c. 1715-20, 9 bays and 2 storeys with attic above cornice, in brick with stone dressings. 3-bay centre with 2 giant columns and 2 giant piers, all Corinthian. Pedimented windows to ground floor.

Ingestre, Staffordshire. *Church* (88), by Sir Christopher Wren for Walter Chetwynd, 1673-6. Nave and aisle church with W tower and fittings of great quality, especially plasterwork.

Ingleby, Derbyshire. *Ingleby Toft,* brick house of early C18 with hipped roof and dormers and slightly projecting central bay topped by pedimented attic.

Innes House, Grampian Region. (34.) 1640-53 by William Aytoun. L-plan

house in similar style as Heriot's Hospital. Large stair in angle of L. Segmental and high-pointed pediments over fairly regular fenestration.

Ipswich, Suffolk. *Sparrowe's House,* timber-frame house remodelled c. 1670. Over-hanging upper floor plastered and pargetted with oriel windows. *2 St Peter's St,* 9 bays, c. 1700, brick with quoins and a modillioned frieze. *Unitarian Meeting House,* 1699-1700 by Joseph Clarke, carpenter, of 5 bays with 2 storeys and hipped roof. Very fine galleried interior.

Itchen Abbas, Hampshire. *Abbey House,* typical house of 1693, 5 bays with 3-bay pediment on cornice and 2 storeys.

Iver Grove, Buckinghamshire. (62.) Red brick house of 1722-4, perhaps by John James, with pilastered frontispiece and giant pilastered arches on sides supporting arched chimneys.

Kelty House, Tayside Region. Plain T-plan house, 1712.

Kempsford, Gloucestershire. *Reevey Gate Cottages,* random rubble, late C17.

Kemsing, Kent. *St Clere,* 1633, compact brick house similar to Chevening, Kent, but with odd corner turrets. Good staircase.

Kibworth, Leicestershire. *Old House,* 1678, with hipped roof and dormers. Additions 1862.

Kilbirnie, Strathclyde Region. *Church,* gallery added at back of church for Garnock family, between 1703 and 1708. Wood, Classical with beautifully carved bow to front and cornice.

Kimbolton, Cambridgeshire. (57.) Remodelled for 1st Duke of Manchester by Vanbrugh, 1707-10, portico probably by Alessandro Galilei, 1718-9. Staircase painted by Pellegrini.

Kingham, Oxfordshire. *Rectory,* late C17 5-bay house of 2 storeys, with hipped roof. Altered internally c. 1770.

King's Lynn, Norfolk. *Custom's House* (113, *114*), 1683, by Henry Bell, 2 storeys, ground floor with blind arcades, topped by hipped roof and cupola. *Duke's Head Inn,* Henry Bell, c. 1684, large town inn, with gigantic broken segmental cornice pediment.

Kings Weston, Avon. (45, 57.) For Sir Edward Southwell by Vanbrugh, 1712-4. Interior altered by Robert Mylne, 1763-8.

Kingscliffe, Northamptonshire. *Almshouses,* 1668.

Kingsey, Buckinghamshire. *Tythrop*

House, late C17, brick, with staircase with balustrade panels of openwork foliage.

Kingston Bagpuize, Oxfordshire. *House*, c. 1710–20, red brick with stone dressings, with 3-bay attic and pediment. *Rectory*, 1723, by Dr George Clarke of All Souls, Oxford.

Kingston Lacy, Dorset. For Sir Ralph Bankes by Sir Roger Pratt, 1663–5. Considerably altered inside and out by Barry, 1835–9. (National Trust.)

Kingston Russel House, Dorset. Built before 1739, with attached portico of Ionic columns and pediment and rather Vanbrughian Palladian windows unadorned and round-headed.

Kinlet Hall, Shropshire. By Francis Smith, 1727–9, 2 storeys with ½ storey above cornice and 3-bay recess on garden front. Good staircase. Library added 1827.

Kinross House, Tayside Region. (*38, 39*.) By Sir William Bruce for himself, 1686–93.

Kirby Hall, Northamptonshire. Alterations to earlier house, probably by Nicholas Stone, 1638–40, including remodelling of N range in half-understood Classicism.

Kirkcaldy, Fife Region. *Dunnikier House*, 1692, L-plan house with regularised windows and pedimented dormers.

Kirkleatham, Cleveland. *Free School* (*105*) (now Old Hall), 1708–9, 7 bays and 2 storeys with attic. Grand Tuscan doorway.

Kirkoswald, Cumbria. *Ona Ash*, 1693, house and byre of squared and coursed rubble.

Kislingbury, Northamptonshire. *Rectory*, c. 1710, 5 bays and 2 storeys with quoins and hipped roof.

Knutsford, Cheshire. *Presbyterian Chapel* (now Unitarian), 1689, Jacobean vernacular.

Lacock, Wiltshire. *Red Lion Hotel*, early C18, brick with pedimented centre, giant pilasters and segmentally-headed windows.

Lamport, Northamptonshire. *All Saints*, Isham Chapel, 1672, separated from chancel by 3 arches. Good rococo plasterwork in chancel, 1743, during general rebuilding work by William Smith. Monument to Sir Justinian Isham by Francis Smith, 1730. *Hall* (*28*), by John Webb for Sir Justinian Isham,

1655–7, wings by Francis Smith, 1732–40. (Open to the public.) *Rectory*, Francis Smith, 1727–30, containing good staircase and panelling.

Lancaster, Lancashire. *Judge's Lodging*, 1675, early symmetrical arrangement of 7 bays and 3 storeys, doorway odd with a broken segmental pediment on thin Tuscan columns.

Langford Manor, Wiltshire. 5-bay, 3-storey entrance front added (1713) to earlier house.

Langton-by-Partney, Lincolnshire. *St Peter and St Paul*, c. 1720–30, red brick church with odd octagonal bell-turret.

Lauder, Borders Region. *Church* (*98*), 1673, by Sir William Bruce for 1st Duke of Lauderdale, rather odd part-traditional, part-Classical building, cross-shaped with central octagonal tower.

Leadenham Old Hall, Lincolnshire. Stone Williamite house of 1690s.

Leasingham, Lincolnshire. *Ancient House*, 1655, small vernacular manor house.

Ledstone Hall, West Yorkshire. Mid C17 3-winged and gabled house.

Leeds, West Yorkshire. *St John* (*75, 76, 161*), 1632–3, minimal Perpendicular church with central arcade dividing nave and extremely fine fittings. *Austhorpe Hall*, 1694, 2 storeys with hipped roof.

Lees Court, Kent. (*67*.) 13-bay, 2-storey block with giant Ionic order and deep eaves-cornice, c. 1640. Related to Lindsey House, Lincoln's Inn Fields, and others of Jonesian townhouse type.

Leeswood, Clwyd. *The Black Gates*, early C18, between Lodges. *The White Gates*, screen only. *House*, early C18 with pilastered front, now rendered, and wings, now removed. Switzer garden with avenues and mound survives.

Leicester, Leicestershire. *Belgrave Hall*, c. 1710, house with gables in red and blue brick chequer.

Leighton Bromswold, Cambridgeshire. *St Mary* (*75*), restored early English church with C17 tower and other additions by poet, George Herbert. Tower gothic in spirit but with Classical details such as arches of belfry openings and windows.

Leintwardine, Hereford and Worcester. *Heath House*, U-shaped house of c. 1650 with pitched roof, cross windows and prominent chimney and breast.

Leith Hall, Grampian Region. Much

altered L-plan tower-house, 1650.

Lennoxlove, Lothian Region. For 1st Duke of Lauderdale by Sir William Bruce, 1673–4 and 1676–7.

Leslie Castle, Grampian Region. Large ruined L-plan house, 1661–3, with corbelled turrets, no regular fenestration and large square-newel stair in angle of L.

Lichfield, Staffordshire. *Bishop's Palace,* 1686–7, by Edward Pierce, only sizeable episcopal palace to be built in Britain during the period. Ashlar-faced with hipped roof and 3-bay central cornice-pediment.

Lilford, Northamptonshire. *Hall,* S front of 1635, 9 bays with bow windows flanking. N side of 1656, altered 1711, with good interiors of 1730 including Entrance Hall by Henry Flitcroft, and staircase.

Lincoln, Lincolnshire. *Cathedral,* Honywood Library, 1674, in style of Wren, with Tuscan cloister. *Friend's Meeting House,* 1689, very early vernacular. *St Giles,* formerly St Peter-at-Arches, by Francis and William Smith, c. 1720–4, dismantled 1932, rebuilt in suburbs 1936. Restored by S. S. Teulon, 1853–4. Brick church very similar to those at Burton-on-Trent and Whitchurch.

Linton House, Cambridgeshire. Garden front, c. 1710, with projecting wings and oddly wide windows. Good staircase.

Linton-in-Craven, North Yorkshire. *Fountaine's Hospital,* 1720, Wakefield-like block with wings and 2-storey cupola-ed centrepiece with monumental doorway surmounted by niche in form of Venetian window with blank side-lights.

Little Gidding, Cambridgeshire. *St John the Evangelist,* tiny church renovated for community set up by Nicholas Ferrar (1626). Façade of 1714 with large doorway between rusticated angle-pilasters under belfry with obelisk pierced by 3 rectangular openings (probably referring to the Trinity).

Liverpool, Merseyside. *Croxteth hall,* W front added by Richard Molyneaux, 1702, brick with stone dressings, rather strange spacing of windows and panel of trophies over door. *Blue Coat School* (now Bluecoat Chambers), 1717, H-shaped with hall and chapel in centre, 2 storeys with large arched windows.

Llangarren, Hereford and Worcester. *Langstone Court,* c. 1700, typical Queen Anne smaller house. Good plasterwork inside.

Llanrwst, Clwyd. *Parish church,* Gwydir chapel, 1633–4. Gothic with Classical doorway.

Lockleys House, Hertfordshire. Red brick house, 1717, attic above cornice.

Logie, Fife Region. *Church,* by Thomas Bachop, 1684, traditional vernacular Gothic.

St John, Leeds, West Yorkshire, 1632–33. Divided nave interior with over-restored Jacobean screen

LONDON

City of London

St Paul's Cathedral (82, 84, *84*, 85, *85*, 86, *86*, 87, *163*), built by Sir Christopher Wren, between 1675 and 1710. Screen removed 1860. Dome decorated by Sir James Thornhill, choir stalls by Gibbons, 1696–8. *Great Model* (82, 83, *83*), now in Model Room at St Paul's. Designed by Wren, 1673–4. *St Andrew, Holborn* (79), Holborn Circus, Wren, 1684–92, tower, 1704, bombed 1941, restored 1961. Galleried hall-church with W tower; belfry openings among only baroque features of City churches, with partly broken segmental arch set inside larger and heavier rounded arch-opening. *St Andrew-by-the-Wardrobe* (*162*), Queen Victoria St, Wren, 1685–95, bombed 1940, restored 1961 by Marshall Sisson. Rectangular church with arched

windows, plain tower and galleries on 3 sides. No fittings survive. *St Anne and St Agnes* (80), Gresham St, Wren, 1676–87, bombed 1940, restored 1966. Square exterior, ends of arms of Greek cross pedimented and voluted. Inside low central dome supported by 4 Corinthian columns. *St Benet's Welsh Church*, Queen Victoria St, Wren, 1677–85. Small rectangular church with side galleries, with many original fittings. *St Bride, Fleet St* (78, 82), Wren, 1670–84, spire, 1701–3, bombed 1940, restored 1957, sadly with seating facing inwards and over-dominant altarpiece. Plain hall-church with doubled columns supporting the galleries, which were destroyed during 2nd World War. Very good spire of diminishing octagons. *Christ Church, Newgate Street* (79, 82), Wren, 1677–91, steeple, 1703–4, bombed 1940, tower and ruins remain. *St Clement, Eastcheap*

St Andrew-by-the-Wardrobe, Queen Victoria Street, London, 1685–95; Sir Christopher Wren. Typically simple example of a City church exterior

St Paul's Cathedral, 1675–1710; Sir Christopher Wren. Dome and west towers

(78), King William St, Wren, 1683–7. Oblong with small S aisle, unassuming exterior, some original fittings including excellent pulpit. *St Dunstan-in-the-East* (82), Idol Lane, Eastcheap, only tower survives, Wren, 1702. His most magnificent Gothic work, spire topping tower carried on 4 buttresses diagonally between corner pinnacles. *St Edmund, King and Martyr*, Lombard Street, Wren, 1670–9, spire, 1706–7. Tower over main S front, which has central cornice-pediment. Simple rectangular nave without aisle. *St James, Garlickhythe* (80, *80*), Upper Thames St, Wren, 1674–87, damaged 1940, restored 1963. Nave and aisle church with clerestory and deep chancel, now divorced from its surroundings by traffic in Upper Thames St. Fine fittings. *St Katherine Creechurch* (75, *76*), Leadenhall St, 1628–31. Nave and aisle interior with cusped clerestory windows, traceried vaulting and E rose window, but Corinthian arcade. *St Lawrence Jewry* (78, 89), Gresham St, Wren, 1670–87, bombed 1940, restored 1957. Rectangular nave with N aisle and vaulted ceiling above clerestory. Arched windows and giant Corinthian order. *St Magnus the Martyr* (78, 82), Lower Thames St, Wren, 1671–87, steeple, 1703–6. Tower with domed octagon above. Barrel-vaulted nave divided from aisles by fluted Ionic columns. *St Margaret, Lothbury*, Wren, 1686–93, steeple, 1698–1700. Irregular parallelogram in plan with clerestory of round windows and very fine fittings. *St Margaret Pattens* (78), Eastcheap, Wren, 1684–9, steeple 1689–1701. Clerestoried rectangle with N aisle and W gallery carrying organ. *St Martin, Ludgate Hill* (80), Wren, 1677–87. One of the most imaginative of City churches, the interior converted into Greek cross by 4 central columns and 4 sections of entablature in corners of space. Tower and lead-covered spire are essential part of view up Ludgate Hill towards St Paul's. *St Mary Abchurch* (81), Cannon St, Wren, 1681–7, bombed 1940, restored. Walls with arched windows topped by round ones. Interior given appearance of being regular by painted dome carried on pendentives, decorated by William Snow, after 1708. *St Mary Aldermary*, Bow Lane, Wren, 1682, tower, 1701–4. Gothic Wren church, nave and aisles, ceilings decorated with

sumptuous plaster Perpendicular fan-vaulting. Some surviving C17 fittings. *St Mary-at-Hill* (78, 80, 88), Lovat Lane, Eastcheap, Wren, 1670–6 and later. Splendid interior with original fittings in Greek cross shape with 4 columns in centre of space. Victorianised by James Savage, 1843. *St Mary-le-Bow* (78, 82, *82*), Cheapside, Wren, 1670–83, bombed 1941, restored 1964. Barrel-vaulted nave with giant Corinthian order. *St Mary Woolnoth* (89, 92, *165*), Lombard St, Hawksmoor, 1716–27, fittings rearranged during William Butterfield's restoration (1876). Tower massive, with banded rustication below, supporting columned belfry stage above, all topped by 2 further rectangles, with balustrades. Interior square with 3 columns at each corner of clerestory, and which used to support galleries. *St Michael, Cornhill* (89), Wren, 1670–7, tower by Hawksmoor, 1718–24. Restored by Sir George Gilbert Scott, 1857–60. *St Michael Paternoster Royal*, Wren, 1686–94, steeple, 1715–7, bombed 1944, restored 1968. *St Nicholas Cole Abbey*, Queen Victoria St, Wren, 1671–81, bombed 1941, restored 1962. Simple rectangle with W gallery. *St Peter, Cornhill* (79), Wren, 1677–87. Barrel-vaulted nave and side aisles divided by piers faced by pilasters. Good fittings. *St Stephen Walbrook* (80, 81, *81*, 82), Wren, 1672–7, steeple, 1717, bombed 1941, restored 1954. Sumptuous interior with much plasterwork, especially coffering of dome. *St Vedast, Foster Lane* (78, 82, *82*), Wren, 1695–1700, steeple, 1709–12, bombed 1940, restored 1962. Simple rectangle with S aisle. Tower Baroque, with alternating convex and concave sides, diminishing to obelisk-like spire. *Amen Court*, 1–3, late C17 brick houses. *Apothecaries Hall*, Blackfriars Lane, 1669–71, street front 1684, much altered. *Chapter House*, (St Paul's Cathedral), Dean's Court, Wren, 1712–4, brick house with rubbed dressings. *College of Arms* (115, 116), Queen Victoria St, 1671–88, plain brick block with Ionic pilaster order emphasising centres of wings. Very fine set of gates. *4 Creechurch Place*, early C18 brick townhouse. *Deanery, Dean's Court*, Wren, 1670, plain brick house for Dean of St Paul's. *Laurence Pountney Hill, 1 & 2*, 1703, 4-storey Queen Anne brick

St Mary
Woolnoth,
Lombard Street,
London, 1716–27;
Nicholas
Hawksmoor.
Strongly
sculptured tower,
typical of
Hawksmoor, to a
small church

houses. *Laurence Pountney Lane, 7a & 9,* later C17 brick houses. *72 Leadenhall Market,* late C17, brick. *Monument,* Fish Street Hill, Hooke with Wren, 1671–6. Memorial to Great Fire, column topped by finial representing fire. Base decorated with relief by Caius Gabriel Cibber, 1674. *St Bartholomew's Hospital,* Smithfield, Gateway, Edward Strong, 1702–3. 2 storeys and attic, flanked by giant Ionic pilasters carrying full-width top pediment, above rusticated archway.

Central niche above arch with aedicule of doubled columns and broken segmental pediment containing statue of Henry VIII. *Temple, King's Bench Walk,* 1678, brick. *Temple, Middle Temple Gate,* Roger North, 1684, with giant Ionic pilaster order supporting full-width pediment. *Temple, Middle Temple Lane, 2 & 3,* c. 1693, brick with very late example of timber-faced jetties above. *Vintner's Hall,* Upper Thames St, Edward Jarman, 1671. Much altered but restored. Panelled Hall

165

with good carved decoration and screen set back against wall. Good carved staircase. *Wardrobe Place*, *3–5*, c. 1710, close containing pair of small Queen Anne houses. *8 Wormwood St*, early C18, 3-bay townhouse.

City of Westminster

St Clement Danes, Strand (95), Wren, 1680–2, upper part of tower by James Gibbs, 1719–20. Bombed 1941, restored 1957–8. Aisled church with galleries and chancel made to appear deeper by perspective coffering in coved ceiling. *St George, Hanover Square*, John James, 1720–5, restored by Benjamin Ferrey, 1871. Large but simple galleried hall, with hexastyle portico and tower behind it on an attic-base. *St James, Piccadilly* (79, *79*, 89), Wren, 1676–84, bombed 1940, restored 1947–54. The quintessential Wren-church: large, light and simple. Wide nave and galleried aisles with tower at end. Very similar to St Andrew, Holborn, and basis for development of eighteenth-century Anglican church. *St John, Smith Square* (89, *90*, 92), Thomas Archer, 1713–28, gutted 1941, restored for use as concert hall. One of Fifty New Churches Commission buildings. Main entrances to N and S emphasised by huge porticos with broken rectangular pediments, flanked by oval columned towers set back. E and W arms project from body of church, which is only visible from outside in convex walls between arms of cross, and are topped by pedimented attics. Interior with large central square between 2 entrances, delineated by columns. *St Martin-in-the-Fields* (97, *97*), James Gibbs, 1722–6. Body of church in form of temple with giant hexastyle portico set back, behind and above which is tower carrying octagon and spire. Ends of sides given extra emphasis by doubling of order as full columns and piers either side of recessed end bays. Nave and aisle interior divided into 3 by giant Corinthian columns carrying arches which are springing of sumptuously plastered barrel-vault (stuccoists, Artari and Bagutti). *St Mary-le-Strand* (94), James Gibbs, 1714–7. Simple oblong church articulated in 2 storeys inside and out. Fine plasterwork ceiling inside. *St Paul, Covent Garden* (76, *77*, 94), Inigo Jones, 1631–3. Originally brick, refaced with Portland stone, 1788–9. Gutted

1795, rebuilt by Thomas Hardwick, 1796–8. Altered internally by William Butterfield, 1871–2. Refaced in brick, 1887–8. Very plain, most monumental architectural feature of which is portico at E end, doorway of which is blank. Hugely overhanging eaves-cornice. Simple hall interior. *Westminster Abbey* (89), W towers, Nicholas Hawksmoor, 1734, completed by John James, c. 1745. Most self-effacing of Hawksmoor's Gothic works, repeating motifs of lower part but with stronger emphasis on horizontals and verticals. *Ashburnham House* (39, 68), attributed to John Webb, before 1662, for William Ashburnham. Plain brick block containing excellent top-lit square-newel staircase. *Banqueting House* (23, 24, *24*, 25, *25*, 85), *Whitehall*, Inigo Jones, 1619–22, exterior progressively refaced in Portland stone, 1774, 1785 and 1828. *Bedford Chambers*, Covent Garden, Henry Clutton, 1877–9, near copy of part of 1 side of Piazza, originally built by Inigo Jones and Isaac de Caus 1631–7. Tall rusticated and arched ground-floor and upper floor divided by rustications. *Bluecoat School* (*105*), Caxton St, 1709, 2-storey façade with central 1st floor niche and clock above cornice topped by broken segmental pediment. (National Trust.) *Buckingham House* (59), St James's, William Winde, 1702–5, for Duke of Buckingham. Altered and enlarged by Sir William Chambers, 1762–9, and subsequently enlarged by Nash, Blore and Aston Webb to become Buckingham Palace. 9-bay house of 2 storeys with attic above cornice and centre emphasised by giant pilaster order. *Greycoat School*, Greycoat Place, 1701, plain 3-storey brick building with dormers, main entrance set in central windowless projection with 2 1st-floor niches either side of coat-of-arms. *Russell House*, 43, King St, Covent Garden, attributed to Thomas Archer, 1716–7. Characteristic swept up cornice related to Chicheley. *St James's Palace*, Queen's Chapel, Inigo Jones, 1623–5. Simple coffered hall, at E end Jones's first use of Venetian window (although from outside it appears as arched window set between 2 flat-headed windows). *St James's Palace*, State Apartments, Wren, 1703, for Queen Anne. *St James's Palace*, Stable Yard, Hawksmoor, 1716–7, brick with stone dressings, ground floor arcaded, 1st-floor windows in arched recesses.

Borough of Barking

Bentry Heath House, Wood Lane, Dagenham, timber-framed house, C17.

Borough of Bexley

Hall Place, Bourne Rd, Bexley, very good early Stuart house, mid C17, of brick with stone dressings. In fact, it is 3 wings added to earlier house, with steep hipped roofs and dormers. Ground-floor windows were placed in shallow, arched recesses; on W front bay rhythm was broken up by use of oval windows.

Borough of Bromley

Bromley College (99, 104), High St, 1670–2 by Captain Richard Rider for John Warner, Bishop of Rochester. Large quadrangle with 17-bay façade with projecting wings and large 2-storey entrance arch.

Borough of Camden

St George, Bloomsbury (92, 93, 94, 167), Nicholas Hawksmoor, 1716–31, restored by G E Street, 1871. Pedimented hexastyle portico leading into main rectangular central space with clerestory above. Tower set back to left of portico with quadruple porticoed temple above, then row of swags and finally tall stepped pyramid supporting statue of King George. *Chapel*, Lincoln's Inn, c. 1619–23, in a mixed Gothic-Classical style, with Perpendicular Gothic predominating. *44, Lincoln's Inn Fields*, c. 1702. Simple brick-fronted house, with flat-headed sashes and stone quoins and string-courses. *Gray's Inn Square*, Holborn, 1676–88. Typical townhouses of 4 storeys in brick with pitched roofs. *Lindsey House* (67, 67, 68), Lincoln's Inn

St George, Bloomsbury, London, 1716–31; Nicholas Hawksmoor. A square clerestory heightens the dual axes

Fields, c. 1640, for Sir David Cunningham, possibly by Nicholas Stone. Only survivor of several houses of this type (3 storeys with applied pilaster order), in this area, including houses on S side of Great Queen St, (c. 1640, by Peter Mills, demolished). *New Square*, Lincoln's Inn, containing best selection of houses of c. 1690 in London, all to similar design. *New Square Gateway*, Lincoln's Inn, to Carey St, 1697, with 4-centred arch. *14 Took's Court*, c. 1720, simple 3-storey front with deep cornice supported on flanking Ionic pilasters.

Borough of Croydon

Ruskin House, Coombe Rd, early C18, typical of Queen Anne interlude before onset of Georgian, with pilasters instead of quoins and segment-headed windows.

Borough of Ealing

Boston Manor, Brentford, brick Jacobean house of c. 1622–3 given appearance of artisan mannerism by alterations of c. 1670. Windows probably later.

Borough of Enfield

Clarendon Arch, Enfield, tunnel taking Salmons Brook under New River. Dated 1682 on inscription. *Gentlemen's Row*, 9–23, row of early C18 townhouses.

Borough of Greenwich

St Alfege (92, 94, *94*), Greenwich High Rd, Nicholas Hawksmoor, 1712–18, upper part of steeple, John James, 1730. Temple with transepts and W tower. E front faces street with portico in antis, central bay arching up into pediment. Galleried interior with large oval frame to ceiling. *Albury Street*, *13–43* (odd excluding 21), Deptford, 1705–c. 1717, designed and partly built by Thomas Lucas of Deptford. 2- and 3-storey houses of purple brick with red dressings. Good doorcases, interiors and staircases. *Arsenal*, Woolwich, buildings for Royal Board of Ordnance, including Dial Square (*117*, 118), 1717; the Old Foundry (117), 1717; and Old Board of Ordnance (117, *118*), 1718–20. *Eltham Lodge* (33, *169*), Court Rd, for Sir John Shaw by Hugh May, 1663–4, small house of 7 bays with hipped roof in brick, with central pediment supported by Ionic pilasters. Very Dutch, based on such buildings as Mauritshuis in the Hague (Jacob van Campen, begun 1633), or the

St Sebastiaansdoelen in the Hague (Arent van's Gravesande, 1636). Very good staircase inside, with balustrade of carved floral panels. *Garden Pavilion*, Charlton House, Charlton (now public convenience), sometimes attributed to Inigo Jones, c. 1630. Charming little pilastered brick building with concave-sided pyramid roof. *Gazebo*, The Grange, Croom's Hill, possibly by Robert Hooke, c. 1672. *Greenwich Hospital*, 1696 onwards (65, 100, *100*, 101, *102*). Sir Christopher Wren designed general plan as Surveyor (until 1716). He also personally designed King Charles base block, Great Hall, domes and colonnades. Hawksmoor (Clerk of Works, 1698–1735) built Queen Anne base block (103), begun 1701, and King William base block (101, 102, *102*), begun 1698. Later work by Thomas Ripley, including completion of Queen Mary block (101, 102), c. 1735. James Stuart rebuilt Chapel, 1780–8. Great Hall was decorated by Sir James Thornhill, 1708–12. *Greenwich Hospital*, King Charles Block (42, *42*, 45, 101, 103), John Webb, 1664–9, included here separately from rest of Hospital as it was begun earlier as part of planned new palace for Charles II. *Manor House*, Croom's Hill, 1695. *Morden College* (100, *100*, *169*), Kidbrooke Grove, Greenwich, attributed to Edward Strong, 1695. *Park Hall*, Croom's Hill, John James, 1717–9, much altered later. *Queen's House* (15, 23, *24*, 101), Romney Rd, Inigo Jones, 1616–9, for Queen Anne of Denmark, finished 1630–5 for Queen Henrietta Maria. Altered 1661, almost certainly not by Webb, when bridges to W and E of central spine were added. *Ranger's House*, Chesterfield Walk, c. 1690 by Andrew Snape. Substantially rebuilt during C18. Central block original, with 3-bay central recess with windows more closely spaced than segment-headed ones of 2-bay wide wings. 2 storeys with balustraded parapet. Plum brick with red dressings, stone string-courses. *Royal Observatory*, Greenwich Park, Sir Christopher Wren, 1675–6. A peculiar little building by virtue of specialised purpose. The N façade is flat with 3 tall windows above basement, parapet with flanking square-domed towers. Facing S it has 5 sides, around main chamber. Flat roof to allow use of largest telescope slung from mast

Eltham Lodge, Greenwich, 1663–64; Hugh May's version of the post-Restoration house with pilasters, a Dutch motif

Morden College, Blackheath, 1695; possibly by Edward Strong. A wide, rather low post-Restoration block masking the courtyard behind

to S of Observatory. 66 *Croom's Hill*, probably 1630–44, artisan mannerist house characteristic of SE, especially Kent. *Vanbrugh Castle*, Maze Hill, originally part of complex of houses by Vanbrugh in this area, all built after 1718 but now demolished except for Vanbrugh Castle. Typical of Vanbrugh's later style, solid brick house with round and square towers, machicolations, heavy mouldings and deep recesses.

Borough of Hackney
Geffrye Almshouses (103) (now Geffrye Museum), Shoreditch, 1710, very similar to Morden Hospital.

Borough of Harrow
Whitchurch. St Lawrence, John James, 1714–6. *Pinner House*, Pinner. Baroque brick house, 1721.

Borough of Havering
Morris Dancer Public House, Newhall Harold Rd, Romford, early C18, brick house of 5 bays and 2 storeys with dormers and segment-headed windows.

Borough of Hillingdon
Swakeleys House (14, 15, *15*), for Edmund Wright, 1630.

Borough of Islington
Cromwell House, Highgate Hill, c. 1637–8. *New River Head*, Finsbury, headquarters of Metropolitan Water Board, containing windmill and house-mill (c. 1708) as well as later buildings. Also 1609–13 revetment of the *Round Reservoir* of the New River.

Royal Borough of Kensington and Chelsea
Chelsea Hospital (100, 101, *101*), Royal Hospital Rd, Kensington, Sir Christopher Wren, 1682–92. *Holland House*, Holland Park, *Gate-piers*, originally to forecourt of house, Nicholas Stone, 1629. Pair of columned and pedimented aedicules containing niches. *Kensington Palace, King's Gallery*, Nicholas Hawksmoor, 1695–6. 2-storeyed brick block with basement and hipped roof, centre emphasised not only by articulation of central 3 bays by pilaster-strips but also by use of panelled attic parapet topped with urns over these 3 bays. *Orangery*, Kensington Palace, Hawksmoor, 1704–5. Complicated but

extremely well-balanced 1-storey brick garden-house.

Borough of Lewisham
St Paul, Deptford (89, *91*, 92, *92*), Deptford Church St, Thomas Archer, 1713–28. Church consisting of temple bisected transversely by another without pediments, W end emphasised by semicircular portico at base of steeple. Corners of interior are enclosed thereby strengthening dual axiality of space, though transepts are still colonnaded as remnants of aisles, and contain galleries. *Albury St, 34–40*, Deptford (see under Greenwich).

Borough of Richmond-upon-Thames
St Mary, Twickenham, 1713–15, John James rebuilt whole church except tower. *Dutch House*, Kew, 1631. Splendid compact 3-storey house with attic close to dividing line between Jacobean and artisan mannerism. Reputedly among first houses in country to use Dutch gable (curving sides topped by pediment), and Flemish bond brickwork. *Ham House* (33), Petersham. Earlier house remodelled for 1st Duke and Duchess of Lauderdale, 1672–4. Extremely fine interiors, recently restored, including staircase with panelled balustrade of military motifs. *Hampton Court Palace* (42, 43, *43*), Sir Christopher Wren, S and E wings, 1689–95, for William and Mary. William Talman continued work on King's Apartment, 1699–1702. *Maids of Honour Row*, Richmond, terraced houses of 5 bays and 3 storeys in brick, 1724. *Orleans House, Octagon*, James Gibbs, 1720. Main surviving feature of house, with splendid rather continental plasterwork by Artari and Bagutti. *Sudbrooke Lodge*, Petersham, by James Gibbs for Duke of Argyll and Greenwich, 1728. 9 bays and 2 storeys, with 3-bay wings, very understated, parapet and much more monumental 3-bay central block, articulated by Corinthian columns and carrying entablature and balustraded parapet. Large central cube room with doubled pilasters and very good plasterwork, possibly by Artari and Bagutti. *Trumpeter's House*, Richmond, c. 1701. Brick with portico standing on paired Tuscan columns and separate pediments over end bays of block.

Borough of Sutton
Carshalton House, West St, Carshalton.
1696–1713 for Edward Carleton. Corner
room with arcading, c. 1720 for Sir John
Fellowes. House of yellow and red brick,
9 bays by 7, 2 storeys with attic above
cornice and angle pilasters. Altered
internally c. 1750. Corner room may
have been work of Henry Joynes who
built powerfully baroque *Water Pavilion*
in garden, c. 1725.

Borough of Tower Hamlets
Christ Church, Spitalfields (92, *93*, 94,
95), Hawksmoor, 1716–31. *St Anne,
Limehouse*, Nicholas Hawksmoor,
1714–30. Extremely monumental and
complex exterior with W tower over
buttressed apsidal entrance. Large
galleried interior with recessed chancel
and columned corner inserts giving
minimum lateral emphasis not unlike
those at Wren's St Martin, Ludgate Hill.
One of great churches of London; must it
stay derelict? *St George-in-the-East* (92),
Wapping Stepney, Hawksmoor,
1714–29. Gutted 1941, restored as shell
containing church, church hall and
rectory, 1960–4. Exterior basically
temple, but with corner towers and
turrets and side recesses. Very heavy W
tower base surmounted by buttressed
octagon. Interior had groin-vaulted
centre with shallow arched arms, giving
greater cross-axial emphasis than most
other churches. *Raine's House*, Raine St,
1719. 4 Corinthian pilasters and 2 niches
at 1st-floor level showing original
purpose as school. *37 Stepney Green*,
1692–94. A detached townhouse of
redbrick, 2 storeys, 5 bays, with
dormers. *Trinity Ground* (103),
Almshouses and Chapel, Mile End Road,
1695, by William Ogbourne. 2 ranges
facing each other, red brick with 1 storey
of basement, with hipped roofs and
central pediment. Chapel at 1 end with
basement, steps to segmentally
pedimented door. Brick with stone
quoins with pediment across whole of 3-
bay façade, topped by cupola.

Borough of Wandsworth
Roehampton House (62), Wandsworth.
Thomas Archer, 1710–2, extended by
Lutyens, tactfully but rather insipidly,
1912.

Long Ashton, Avon. *Ashton Court,* S

façade added c. 1635. 13 bays,
eccentrically grouped, (3-2-3-3-2) with
middle 3 bays more widely spaced than
remainder. Ground-floor windows with
triangular and segmental pediments, 1st-
floor windows hooded. Large blank attic
area below roof-balustrade only broken
by round windows over 1st, 3rd, 5th,
6th, 7th, 8th, 9th, 11th and 13th bays.
Longbridge Deverill, Wiltshire. *Thynne
Almshouses*, founded 1655, stone and
gabled.
Longdon, Staffordshire. *Hanch Hall*,
early C18, with good 7-bay front of 2
storeys with 3-bay central pediment.
Some pre-C18 work inside; remodelled
in C19.
Longnor Hall, Shropshire. Rectangular
compact block of 1670s, Coleshill-type,
7 bays and 2 storeys, but with shaped
gable on entrance side.
Loosely Row, Buckinghamshire. *Lacey
Green Windmill*, timber smock mill
originally from Chesham, c. 1650,
moved to present site (1821). Still
contains some C17 wooden machinery.
Lorton, Cumbria. *Hall*, 1663, addition
to pele-tower, an early attempt at
Classical arrangement.
Louth, Lincolnshire. *The Mansion*,
1704, 7 bays and 2 storeys, with narrow
projecting central bay topped by deep
segmental pediment.
Lower Slaughter Manor House,
Gloucestershire. By Valentine Strong,
c. 1640–50, exterior altered during C19.
Interiors contemporary with building of
house, including good plaster ceiling and
2 good fireplaces.
Lowesby Hall, Leicestershire. Early
C18 house with 9-bay entrance front and
11-bay garden front. Entrance hall ceiling
painted, possibly by Verrio. Altered and
extended by Lutyens, c. 1912.
Lowther, Cumbria. *Church*, remodelled
1686, nave, aisles and lower part of
tower, for Sir John Lowther. Very simple
with rectangular windows in aisles and
arched windows in E and W ends.
Altered 1856. Robert Hooke may have
been involved; he certainly made a design
for *Lowther Castle*, c. 1690, not in the
event followed.
Lucton, Hereford and Worcester. *Sir
John Pierrepont's School* (105), 1708, in
most respects similar externally to usual
brick house with stone dressings; 7 bays,
2 storeys with hipped roof and dormers.
3-bay centre carrying cornice-pediment.

Niche above central bay. The building behind not regular.

Lumley Castle, Co. Durham. Vanbrugh may have been responsible for the regularisation of the S and W fronts, 1722. Certainly he decorated Library, with characteristic boldly rusticated pilasters.

Lyddington, Leicestershire. *St Andrew,* communion rails, c. 1635, surrounding altar on all 4 sides; as Pevsner says, compromise between Laudian and Puritan views.

Lydiard Tregoze, Wiltshire. *St Mary,* a small Perpendicular church mostly furnished in C17, including pulpit, screen and very fine communion rail of c. 1700.

Lyme Park, Cheshire. Additions to earlier house by Giacomo Leoni, c. 1725–35. S front monumental with rusticated ground floor and piano nobile and upper floor united by giant order. Giant portico, with balustraded attic in centre above and behind portico added later. Good staircase and excellent panelled saloon in Gibbons tradition, probably remaining from earlier house.

Lyndon, Leicestershire. *Hall,* 1671–3, for Sir Abel Barker by John Sturges. A slightly irregular stone house of 7 bays reminiscent of Thorpe Hall, Cambs., with dormers and mullioned and transomed windows. *Top Hall,* c. 1675–80, more normal post-Restoration house, but still with cross-windows.

Macclesfield, Cheshire. *Unitarian Chapel,* 1689, Jacobean vernacular survival. *Pear Tree House,* Jordangate, 1728, brick house with stone dressings.

Maesmawr Hall, Powys. Timber-framed house built perhaps as late as 1690s.

Manchester, Greater Manchester. *St Ann,* 1709–12, stone with 3 stage tower and 6-bay sides with double tier of arched windows; coupled pilasters. Restored by Alfred Waterhouse, 1886–91.

Mapledurham, Oxfordshire. *Forge Cottage,* 1691, brick with flint dressings.

Mapleton, Derbyshire. *Clergymen's Widows Almshouses,* 1727, brick with stone dressings, 5 bays with 2 storeys, hipped roof. Centre bay projects, flanked by giant rusticated pilasters.

Marlborough, Wiltshire. *College, C House,* 1699–1706, originally built as house for Duke of Somerset, with façade of 15 bays with central recess of 3 bays. Chequered brick wings with rubbed quoins, red brick centre with arched windows and parapet. Interesting interior. *Poulton House,* 1706, chequered brick, 7 bays and 2 storeys with 3-bay pediment. Very good staircase with stucco work.

Marlow, Buckinghamshire. *Marlow Place* (62), Thomas Archer, c. 1720, small brick baroque house, basement and 2 storeys with high parapet, angle pilasters defining central pedimented projections. *Western House,* West St, 1699, 3-bay wide house in chequered brick with entrance hood in shell form.

Marshfield, Avon. *Catherine Wheel Inn,* High St, early C18 with ashlar façade of 2 storeys and 7 bays with balustraded parapet. *The Hospice,* High St, C17, gabled. *Lord Nelson Inn,* High St, early C18, ashlar façade, rusticated quoins and 2 storeys. *Manor House,* early C18, 4 bays and 2 storeys.

Marton Hall, North Yorkshire. Late C17, 5 bays, very good staircase. House altered c. 1806.

Matfield House, Kent. 1728, 7 bays, 2 storeys in red and blue chequer over sandstone basement.

Maugersbury Manor House, Gloucestershire. Begun late C16 and altered 1658. Stone, 3 storeys, L-shaped. Altered in C18.

Mavisbank House, Lothian Region. By William Adam and Sir John Clerk of Penicuik, 1722–c. 1728. Gutted by fire, 1974, shell remains. Odd house with pilaster-like quoins supporting cornice and pediment. Convex roof with flat top and solid balustrade. Decoration between ground and 1st-floor windows and in pediment.

Mawley Hall, Shropshire. (*60, 61.*) For Sir Edward Blount, 1730, possibly by Francis Smith. Red brick with stone dressings, 9 bays by 7, and 2 storeys with attic over cornice. Tuscan pilasters instead of quoins and rather steep pediment over 3-bay central projection. One of most splendid early C18 interiors in Britain, with magnificent plasterwork.

Medbourne, Leicestershire. *School* added as N transept to church, c. 1650.

Melbury Sampford, Dorset. *Melbury House,* 1692, earlier house remodelled by a Mr Watson, with 2 storey N, S and E fronts, parapeted with superimposed orders in 3-bay centres of each side, topped by segmental pediments on sides and triangular pediment on entrance front. Good carving in hall and staircase.

Mellor Hall, Greater Manchester. 7 bay wide house of 1688, with mullioned and transomed windows.

Melton Constable, Norfolk. *Melton Hall* (30), 1664–c. 1670. 9 bays by 7 in brick with stone-faced basement. 3-bay centre projections on garden and entrance fronts carrying pediments. Little remaining of C17 decoration, except ceiling of red drawing-room, plasterwork of high quality (1687). This most beautiful house is now lying empty.

Melville House, Fife Region. (64.) By James Smith for Earl of Melville, 1697–1700.

Meriden Hall, West Midlands. Remodelled by Francis Smith, c. 1720.

Mertoun House, Borders Region. Sir William Bruce for Sir William Scott, 1703. Wings added by William Burn, 1843. Also known as Harden House. Rather Palladian house, but originally less so due to tall chimneys and cupola. Still, the influence of John Webb, particularly in a house like Amesbury, cannot be gainsayed.

Metheringham, Lincolnshire. *Church*, traditional, c. 1600, but with Tuscan columns instead of piers.

Mickleton, Gloucestershire. *Medford House*, c. 1694, with hipped roof and dormers.

Midhurst, West Sussex. *Spreadeagle Inn*, c. 1700, 7 bays, brick with stone dressings.

Milton Malsor, Northamptonshire. *Manor*, early C18 house with painted front and pitched roof.

Minchinhampton, Gloucestershire. *Hyde Court*, C17, 2 storeys and 4 gables, with wooden transoms and mullions. *Old House*, C17, with gables, mullioned windows and diagonally set chimneys. *Market House*, High St, c. 1700, half-hipped roof supported on stone columns with row of wooden columns behind.

Minsterley, Shropshire. *Holy Trinity*, 1689, very singular Classical church with buttresses and arches along sides, and very odd façade on W tower.

Miserden, Gloucestershire. *Hazle House*, early C18, central block topped by eagles, with lower side wings. *Wishanger Farm*, C16/17 gabled farm-house.

Mitcham, Surrey. *Eagle House*, c. 1700, tall house with balustraded roof and cupola.

Mold, Clwyd. *Gwysaney*, plain house, early C17. *Rhual*, brick house, 1634.

Monington-on-Wye, Hereford and Worcester. *Church* (88), 1679–80, nave and chancel, similar to Newent, Gloucs., in style of mixed Gothic-Classical.

Monmouth, Gwent. *St Mary*, nave 1736–7 by F Smith of Warwick. *Great Castle House* (69), 1673 for Marquess of Worcester, large stone house. *St Bride's House*, Monk St, c. 1700. *Town Hall* (113), 1724.

Moor Green, Wiltshire. *Jaggards*, 1657, E-shaped house of odd configuration, with porches in wings. Cross windows and gables.

Moor Park, Hertfordshire. (62, *174*.) Built c. 1720–28, for South Sea Company profiteer Benjamin Styles. According to documentary evidence, it is work of Sir James Thornhill, but it is house in style of Lower Rhine, with arched ground-floor arched windows and banded rustication and use of flat hoods to 1st floor windows. Rather cramped attic windows are also typical of that region, as is great height of block. Giacomo Leoni, whose possible contribution is often disregarded, is only architect who could have known of country houses in that part of Germany; he studied under Count Matteo de Alberti in Düsseldorf, and Moor Park has considerable similarities with that architect's grandiose design for palace in Heidelberg, of 1709 and later.

Morcott, Leicestershire. *Manor House*, 1687, recessed centre with wings and cross-windows.

Moresby Hall, Cumbria. Still under muddled Jones influence at late date of c. 1690–1700. Wholly rusticated 2-storey façade, with not very correct window-pediments.

Morham, Lothian Region. *Church*, 1724, traditional vernacular, but with crude Classical articulation on end of N aisle.

Morpeth, Northumberland. *Town Hall*, for 3rd Earl of Carlisle, by Vanbrugh, 1714. Reconstructed to original design after fire of c. 1875. Simple façade with twin towers and heavy banded rustication.

Morville, Shropshire. *Aldenham Park*, early C18 house, long and low, with stone pitched roof.

Mothecombe House, Devon. Brick house, c. 1710, with deep eaves cornice and angle pilaster-strips.

Moulton, North Yorkshire. *Hall,* late C17, compact gabled house; alternating triangular and segmental 1st-floor window pediments. Staircase with carved panel-balustrade. *Manor,* 1660–70, with 2 short projecting wings enclosing raised terrace. Rather provincial in detail, such as steep triangular pediments to windows.

Moulton Chapel, Lincolnshire. *St James,* octagonal church with unusual domed interior, dated 1722.

Muchelney, Somerset. *Thorney Cottage,* late C17, coursed rubbled, thatched.

Mundham, West Sussex. *Mundham House,* 1671, compact house of 7 bays, with gables.

Murdostoun Castle, Strathclyde. Built for Alexander Inglis by William Adam, c. 1735–40; altered c. 1800.

Myton-upon-Swale, North Yorkshire. *Myton Hall,* late C17, very fine 7 bay and 2 storey rendered brick house with quoins and hipped roof.

Naburn, North Yorkshire. *Bell Hall,* later C17 house, 5 by 3 bays, brick with stone dressings, 2 storeys and hipped roof. Some good interiors.

Nailsworth, Gloucestershire. *Quaker Meeting House,* Chestnut Hill, 1689, simple vernacular exterior with odd arched doorway. Interior contains original furniture. *Barn Close,* Horsley Rd, C17 house, gabled and with wooden mullioned and transomed windows. *Stokes Croft,* Chestnut Hill, C17 house with 3 gables.

Nantwich, Cheshire. *Unitarian Chapel,* 1726, small with large shaped gable. *Almshouses,* 1638.

Nercwys Hall, Clwyd. Brick house, 1638–40. Additions of c. 1815; wings demolished in 1964.

Nether Lypiatt Manor, Gloucestershire. (74.) 2-storey house on basement, with hipped roof and dormers, built 1702–5. Additions by P. Morley Horder, 1923. Very fine wrought iron gates and screen.

Netherhampton House, Wiltshire. Earlier house (c. 1680), but façade and wings added c. 1710–20. Stone-faced, with segment headed windows and 5

Moor Park, Hertfordshire, c.1720–28; probably by Giacomo Leoni. Representative of the Classical side of the continental late baroque

bays and 3 storeys.

Netherton House, Hampshire. Grey brick house with stone dressings, 5 bays and 2½ storeys, dated c. 1720.

Newbattle, Lothian Region. *Church*, by Alexander McGill, 1727–8.

Newbury, Berkshire. *8 Northbrook St*, 1669, brick house, articulated by pilasters on each floor.

Newby Hall, North Yorkshire. 9-bay wide brick house with stone dressings (c. 1700), 2 main storeys and attic below parapet balustrade. Slightly projecting central bay with 1st-floor segmental pediment and further projecting 2-bay wings. Further wings added by Robert Adam, c. 1700–80 to form a sculpture gallery and offices.

Newcastle-upon-Tyne, Tyne and Wear. *Holy Jesus Hospital (99)*, City Rd, 1683, 15 bays wide, double-depth block, 3 storeys high, with very small, rather N European type dormers and arched ground floor. *Surtees House*, C17, 5 storeys high, 5 bays wide, pitched roof and mullioned and transomed windows.

Newent, Gloucestershire. *St Mary (175)*, 1675–9, masons in charge of building,

Francis Jones and James Hill. Mixture of Gothic and Classical motifs, such as use of arched lights in building with internal giant Ionic order round walls. Very wide nave with chancel to 1 side of E end, other side taken up by chapel; gallery down that half of nave.

Newick Park, East Sussex. S front of late C17, using giant pilasters.

Newington Bagpath, Gloucestershire. *Bagpath Court*, c. 1697, 3 bays and 2 storeys with hipped roof.

Newmarket, Suffolk. *King's House*, by William Samwell, 1668–71. Partially demolished after 1814, remains now called Palace House Mansion.

Newport, Essex. *Crown Inn*, 1692, earlier house with interesting late example of pargetting.

Newton Longville, Buckinghamshire. *18 Moor End*, C17 box-frame timber house with use of existing cruck.

Ninfield, East Sussex. *Lower Standard Farm*, 1702, with gables and mullioned and transomed windows.

North Cerney, Gloucestershire. *Rectory*, 1694, stone house with hipped roof.

North Leigh, Oxfordshire. *St Mary*, 2nd

St Mary, Newent, Gloucestershire, 1675–79; Francis Jones and James Hill. A late example, like Monnington, of the mixing of Classical and Gothic motifs

N aisle added in 1687 for James Perrot, with Tuscan internal arcade and windows with arched heads.

North Runcton, Norfolk. *Church*, 1703–13, by Henry Bell, with W tower and square nave with 4 free-standing columns like All Saints, Northampton.

Northampton, Northamptonshire. *All Saints* (88), possibly by Henry Bell, 1677–80. Large town church in Wren style, but with old-fashioned features such as round-headed windows with almost Gothic-type tracery. Portico based on that of Jones's St Paul's, 1701. Interior reminiscent of St Martin, Ludgate Hill, though with centre shallow dome. Statue of Charles II above portico by John Hunt of Northampton.
Session's House, 1676–8, 5 bays with end bays emphasised by attached Corinthian columns and segmental pediments not unlike centrepiece of Royal Exchange in London. Hipped roof and very good plasterwork inside by Edward Goudge, 1684–8.

Northenden, Greater Manchester. *Sharston Hall*, c. 1700, 3 storey red brick house.

Northill, Bedfordshire, *12 Ickwell Green*, small early C18 timber house, partially bricked up.

Norton-in-Hales, Shropshire. *Brand Hall*, c. 1700, brick house with applied portico and deep pediment.

Norwich, Norfolk. *Old Meeting* (now Congregational Chapel), 1693, in brick, 5 bays and 2 storeys, with hipped roof and centre delineated by 4 giant Corinthian columns. Galleried interior.

Nottingham, Nottinghamshire. *St Nicholas*, 1671–82, very typical Wren-influenced church in brick, and Gothic windows in tower. *Castle*, Samuel Marsh, 1674–9 (?), virtually rebuilt as museum by T. C. Hine, 1876–8; rather like Bolsover, with definite Rubens overtones.

Nun Monkton Hall, North Yorkshire. 7-bay, 2-storey house of c. 1690, with hipped roof and giant pilaster order. Good staircase.

Nunnington Hall, North Yorkshire. Probably late C16 house remodelled c. 1680, including S façade with 5-bay gabled centre, and 2 bay wings. some good interiors including late C17 chimney-pieces and staircase.

Nutley, East Sussex. *Windmill*, small open trestle post-mill, probably late C17.

Oakham, Leicestershire. *Hayne House*, Melton Rd, c. 1700, 2 storeys with hipped roof and quoins. *Yule House (177)*, Catmos St, c. 1690, 5 bays, 2 storeys, hipped roof with dormers, brick with stone dressings.

Oakley Hall, Staffordshire. Brick house, 1710, with 3 central bays ashlar-faced, carrying curly gable, more S African looking than anything else. Remodelled c. 1800.

Ockham, Surrey. *Church*, King funerary chapel, c. 1735, attributed to Nicholas Hawksmoor.

Ombersley Court, Hereford and Worcester. 1723–6, perhaps by Francis Smith, for Samuel Sandys. Originally brick with stone dressings, refaced 1812–4 by J. Webb. 7-bay entrance façade of $2\frac{1}{2}$ storeys. Some good interiors including 3 lovely panelled rooms, like those on ground floor at Chicheley. Fine staircase with plaster ceiling.

Orlingbury Hall, Northamptonshire. Brick house with stone dressings and gabled roof, dated 1706 or after.

Oundle, Northamptonshire. *Berrystead*, early C18, large detached stone townhouse. *16 West St*, c. 1660, compact house with deep cornice.

Outwood, Surrey. *Windmill*, the oldest functioning post mill in England, dated 1665.

Over Peover, Cheshire. *Church*, N (Mainwaring) Chapel, c. 1648–50, early Classical chapel. *Stables*, of Hall, 1654, long low brick building with central entrance, and upper floor added later.

Oxford, Oxfordshire. *All Saints* (88, 88), 1707–10, tower, 1718–20, probably by Henry Aldrich. *St Mary-the-Virgin*, doorway, John Jackson, 1637, famous doorway, of curly columns with large segmental pediment, broken and containing dropped aedicular niche. *All Souls College, North Quadrangle (110, 110)*, Nicholas Hawksmoor, 1716–35, symmetrical with two E towers in Hawksmoor's Gothic style. Interiors include Hall, Buttery and Codrington Library, all Classical. *Botanical Garden*, 3 gateways, built by Nicholas Stone, though perhaps not designed by him, 1632–3. Very Italian, in tradition of garden 'grotesque'. *Brasenose College, Chapel and Library*, John Jackson (?), 1656 and after. Chapel mixed Gothic and baroque, very assertive with excellent plaster vault. Also cloister with attached pillars. *Christ Church* (106), Hall staircase, c. 1640. Slim Perpendicular central pier and fan vault, but contemporary 2-flight return stair. Library (108, *109*, 112), Dr George Clarke, 1717–38. Very stately with giant Corinthian half-columns and huge upper cornice. *Peckwater Quadrangle* (108, *109*), Henry Aldrich, 1707–14, early neo-Palladian square, very plain. *Tom Tower* (108, 110), Sir Christopher Wren, 1681–2, over earlier base. *Clarendon Building* (108, 110, *110*), Nicholas Hawksmoor, 1712–5. *Corpus Christi College*, William Townesend built and perhaps designed the *Fellows' Building* and *Cloister*, 1706–12, and the *Gentlemen Commoners' Building*, 1737. *New College, NE block of Garden Quadrangle*, William Townesend, to match Richard Piddington's SE block of 1700. Earliest example of Palladianism in Oxford. *Old Ashmolean Muesum*, Thomas Wood was master-mason,

1678–83. N front to Broad St of 5 bays with close-set transom and mullion windows topped by alternating pediments. Very impressive segmental-pedimented portal facing Sheldonian Theatre, with sumptuous carving by William Bird. *Oriel College, Robinson Buildings*, William Townesend, 1719–20. *Queen's College, Front Quadrangle* (108, *178*), William Townesend, under direction of Dr George Clarke, 1710–21. Very plain, sides arcaded on ground floor and with giant segmental pediments over central 3-bay attic, middle block with giant attached portico topped by cupola, wings with large arched windows on 1 main storey divided by giant pilasters. *Library* (108), 1692–5, 11 bays with rusticated ground floor and arched windows on both floors, though arcade on ground floor was originally open. *Screen* (108), to Hawksmoor's designs modified by Townesend, 1733–6. Rusticated wall with blank arches, topped, in centre, by open cupola. *Williamson Building*, 1671–4,

8 Catmos Street, Oakham, Leicestershire, c. 1690. Typical adaptation of the post-Restoration house as a detached town-house

upper storey added c. 1730, very plain with mullioned and transomed windows. *Radcliffe Camera* (108, 111, *111*), James Gibbs, 1737–48. Probable that Gibbs' design is much indebted to Hawksmoor, who also made designs. *St Edmund Hall*, E range, c. 1680. 5 bays, 2 storeys plus attic with central bay emphasised by giant Ionic columns carrying very steep pediment. *St Giles House*, Bartholomew Peisley the Younger, 1702, with 7-bay stone façade, centre emphasised by 3-bay projection. *St John's College, Canterbury Quadrangle*, built for Archbishop Laud by John Jackson, after 1634. Italian Renaissance in style, with some baroque elements – such as entrance – and some Gothic – such as fan-vaulting in arcade. *Senior Common Room*, Bartholomew Peisley the Elder, 1673–8. Good interior especially plaster-ceiling added by Roberts (1742). *St Michael's St*, 20, *Vanbrugh House* (70, 71), early C18. 5 bays, 3 storeys, the centre bay projecting slightly with pair of giant pilasters carrying very deep cornice. *Sheldonian Theatre* (106, *106*, 107), Sir Christopher Wren, 1664–9. *Stone's Almshouses*, St Clement's, Bartholomew Peisley, 1697 and after. 11 bays and 2 storeys with hipped roof. *Trinity College, Chapel*,

Bartholomew Peisley I or II, 1691–4, possibly to another architect's designs. Very lovely college chapel with beautiful panelling, especially reredos which may have been carved by Gibbons. *Durham Quadrangle*, N range, 1728, by William Townesend, to correspond with N range of garden quadrangle. *Garden Quadrangle*, N block, 1668, by Sir Christopher Wren. *University College, Radcliffe Quadrangle*, Bartholomew Peisley III or William Townesend, 1717–9. *Worcester College, Hall, Chapel* and *Library*, by Dr George Clarke, with assistance from Hawksmoor, begun 1720.

Painswick, Gloucestershire. *Dover House*, Vicarage St, c. 1720, with hipped roof and quoins. *Loveday's House*, now Vicarage, early C18 house with hipped roof and, interestingly, Gibbs surrounds to ground-floor windows. *Old Brownshill*, 2 storey house with gables dated 1665. *Wick Street House*, 1633, of 2 storeys with attics. *Yew Tree House*, Vicarage St, c. 1668, gabled.

Pamphill, Dorset. *High Hall*, c. 1670, 5 bays and 2 storeys on high basement in brick, now rendered. Altered in late C19 and early C20.

Papworth St Agnes, Cambridgeshire.

Queen's College, Front Quad, Oxford, 1710–21; Dr George Clarke and William Townesend. Monumental hall and chapel block between residential wings

Manor House, W front, c. 1700, red brick with blue headers, added to house of c. 1585 and mid-C17. S range, with mullioned and transomed windows and hipped roof.

Parham House, Suffolk. Fragment of house of c. 1630–50, showing use of giant pilasters at early date.

Patterdale, Cumbria. *Hogget Gill Lead Smelter,* very early remains of local lead industry, c. 1630.

Peffermill House, Lothian Region. Plain but regular L-shaped house, 1636, with string-courses and armorial carvings in curved pediment over main doorway.

Pendell House, Surrey. Brick house, 1636, with 3-storey projecting centre bay, ground-floor windows in arched recesses and use of shallow recesses almost like pilaster-strips, with semicircular tabs at top of each.

Penpont House, Powys. House, c. 1666, remodelled 1813. *Dovecot* in park, c. 1720.

Penrith, Cumbria. *Church,* 1720–2, low and solid with very strong pilasters between arched windows and embattled tower from preceding building. 3 galleries inside.

Peterborough, Cambridgeshire.

Guildhall, 1671, 3 by 2 bays, with hipped roof and open ground floor on Tuscan columns and arches.

Petworth House, Sussex. (44, *179.*) Built for Duke of Somerset, c. 1688–90. (National Trust.)

Philorth House, Grampian Region. Single block house of 1666, irregular.

Pickhill House, Clwyd. (61, *180.*) Red brick pilastered house of 1720s.

Pitreavie, Fife Region. (34.) After 1631, large, plain, but regularly fenestrated, tower-house, with recessed centre.

Pitsligo, Grampian Region. *Church, Pitsligo Gallery,* 1634, taking up whole of N aisle.

Plymouth, Devon. *Citadel Gateway,* Sir Bernard de Gomme, 1670. Royal Dockyard, Hamoaze, *The Officer's Dwelling House, Great Storehouse, Ropehouse,* etc., possibly by Robert Hooke, c. 1690–1700. Also *Gun Wharf,* 1718–c. 25, typically Vanbrughian with broken skyline.

Pollok Castle, Strathclyde Region. Late courtyard type house of 1710, though with regular fenestration.

Poole, Dorset. *Westend House,* West St, 1716, 5 bays and 2 storeys with balustraded parapet.

Portesham, Dorset. *Waddon Manor,*

Petworth House, West Sussex, c. 1688–90. The flat Versailles type look is heightened by removal of the dome following fire-damage

1696–1704, 7 bays by 2, 2 storeys with mullioned and transomed windows and hipped roof with dormers.

Portsmouth, Hampshire. *Cathedral, nave,* 1683–93, arcaded in Wren tradition. Plaster ceiling and C17 fittings, including pulpit, restored pews and W gallery (1706). *Broad St, King James Gate,* 1687, moved to present position in Royal Naval Barracks. Much altered and now only an arch, with 2 subsidiaries, flanked by pair of pilasters. *Dockyard, 18 Gun Battery* and *Sally Port,* Bernard de Gomme, c. 1680. *Dockyard Round Tower* and *Frederick's Battery,* 1683 and 1688, re-erected in 1870.

Poulton Manor House, Gloucestershire. 2 storey house, c. 1680, with hipped roof and mullioned and transomed windows.

Powis Castle, Powys. Castle with interiors of C16, C17, C18 and C19, including very fine staircase with carved panelled balustrades of 1670s and state bedroom of same date. Terraces of garden to SE also late C17.

Puddletown, Dorset. *Ilsington House,* c. 1690–1700, 2 storeys with hipped roof. Now rendered and otherwise altered in C19.

Puslinch House, Devon. Brick with stone dressings, 7 bay and 2 storey house of early C18. Hipped roof and 3-bay central projection on entrance front.

Putley, Hereford and Worcester. *The Brainge,* 1703, 5 bays and 2 storeys with hipped roof.

Quatt, Shropshire. *Dudmaston Hall,* for Sir Thomas Wolryche, c. 1695, perhaps by Francis Smith. Altered c. 1820, but remains of Honington-type house visible on entrance-front and inside.

Quendon Hall, Essex. Brick central block of c. 1680 between wing of earlier house, with giant pilasters of irregular rhythm.

Radbourne Hall, Derbyshire. Brick house by William Smith the Younger, 1739, for German Pole. 7 bays and 2 storeys with stone-faced basement. 3 central bays slightly projecting topped by pediment.

Pickhill House, Clwyd, 1720s. West Midlands baroque influence across the border in Wales

Ragley Hall, Warwickshire. (44, 45, *45*, 46.) Built for Earl of Conway by Robert Hooke, 1679–83. Interior altered by Gibbs, c. 1750–5; portico by James Wyatt, c. 1780. 15 bays wide in stone with basement and 2 storeys and balustraded and hipped roof. Library of Hooke period, and Gibbs Great Hall, very baroque with giant pilasters and exquisite plasterwork.

Rainham Hall, Essex. Brick house, c. 1729, with stone quoins and rounded window architraves.

Ramsbury Manor, Wiltshire. Robert Hooke, c. 1680–3, simple house with 2 storeys and cornice-pediment. Hipped roof.

Rattlesden, Suffolk. *Clopton Hall,* 1681, 2-storey timber-framed and plastered house with recessed centre, short wings and hipped roof.

Ravenstone Hall, Leicestershire. Brick house, c. 1725, with 5 bays and 2 storeys and 1-bay cornice-pediment supported on giant Corinthian pilasters.

Raynham Hall, Norfolk. (26, *26*, 27, 30.) For Sir Roger Townshend, begun 1621 but not finished until later 1630s. Built by William Edge, probably to designs by Townshend and Edge, though, as with so many other houses of this date, the involvement of Jones cannot be ruled out. House has been much altered, especially in regularisation of fenestration.

Reigate Priory, Surrey. Painted staircase, 1703, 3-flight newel stair in hall decorated by Verrio.

Ribton Hall, Cumbria. Provincial baroque house by Edward Addison, c. 1690.

Richard's Castle, Hereford and Worcester. *Moor Park,* early C18 house of 11 bays with shaped gables and giant angle pilasters.

Risley, Derbyshire. *Latin House,* c. 1700, originally accommodation for school in village. Hipped roofed house in brick with stone dressings.

Rochdale, Greater Manchester. *Lloyd's Bank,* Lord St, 1708, with pilasters in 2 tiers. *Old Falinge,* Falinge Fold, 1721, rather out-of-date with mullioned and transomed windows.

Rochester, Kent. *Corn Exchange,* 1706, 2-storey brick building with large pediment. *Guildhall,* 1687, open below, standing on Tuscan columns, brick above with hipped roof. Good staircase and

plasterwork in hall.

Rufford Old Hall, Lancashire. New wing, 1662, to earlier black and white house, in brick.

Rye, East Sussex. *Peacocke's School* (103, 104), High St, 1636. Interesting artisan mannerist building in brick with giant order and large pedimented attics. *Lamb House,* West St, 1723. (National Trust.)

Ryston Hall, Norfolk. Built by Sir Roger Pratt for himself 1669–72. 9 bays with a 3-bay centre, but very much altered by Sir John Soane, 1786–8.

St Helen Auckland, Co. Durham. *Saint Helen Hall,* early C18, 2 wings of older house, and coach house, all in Vanbrughian style, though there is no evidence that he was involved.

St Nicholas at Wade, Kent. *1 & 2 Shuart Lane* (*73*), late C17, pair of typical single-stacked vernacular cottages.

Salisbury, Wiltshire. *Collegium Matrarum* (99), built and possibly designed by Thomas Glover of Harnham, Wilts., 1682. *Malmesbury House,* The Close, 7-bay ashlar façade built by 1719 added to earlier house. (Open to the public.) *Mompesson House,* The Close, dated 1701, 7-bay house, ashlar-faced with hipped roof. (National Trust.) *Steynings,* Mill Rd, 1700, 5-bay house with projecting centre bay. *9 The Close,* c. 1675, 5 bays and 2 storeys in brick with good staircase of late C17. *68 The Close* (70, *182*), 1718, ashlar-faced house of 7 bays with attic above cornice and giant pilasters. *Trinity Hospital,* Trinity St, rebuilt 1702, 7 bays and 2 storeys with hipped roof. *Wren Hall,* The Close, formerly Cathedral School, completed 1714, 5 bays of brick on stone basement with quoins and hipped roof.

Sandford Park, Oxfordshire. 5-bay front of c. 1700, with centre bay projecting under pediment enclosing round window.

Satterthwaite, Cumbria. *Stony Hazel Finery Forge,* early C18 forge to rework cast-iron into malleable wrought-iron.

Scole, Norfolk. *White Hart Inn, 1655,* large inn with gables below enormous chimneys and irregular fenestration with panels between windows, created by double order of pilasters.

Scraptoft Hall, Leicestershire. c. 1720. Now Hall of Residence at Leicester Training College. 5 bays and 2 storeys plus attic with giant pilasters framing middle bay and parapet sweeping up towards middle and ends.

Seaton Delaval, Northumberland. (*56, 57.*) Built for Admiral George Delaval by Sir John Vanbrugh, 1720–8. Main block gutted 1822. (Open to the public.)

Sedgefield, Co. Durham. *Church,* splendid Gothic screen and choir-stalls, 1635.

Seend Green House, Wiltshire. c. 1700(?), 7 bays, 3 storeys and parapet.

Send, Surrey. *Worsfold Gates Navigation Lock,* part of Wey Navigation begun 1651, extended 1760. The only original gates to survive.

Selattyn, Shropshire. *Brogyntyn,* Smith-type house of 1735–6, much altered in early C19.

Sevenoaks, Kent. *Bradbourne Farm,* Bradbourne Vale Rd, c. 1700, red and blue brick chequer, 5 bays and 2 storeys

with hipped roof and dormers. *Old House,* High St, c. 1700, red brick house with blue brick chequer, 7 bays and 2 storeys. *Red House,* High St, 1686, red brick, 7 bays, 2 storeys, hipped roof and 1-storey side wings.

Sewerby House, Humberside. Central part, c. 1714, of 7 bays and 2½ storeys, with 3 projecting centre bays. Good interiors, especially staircase.

Sharnbrook House, Bedfordshire. Early C18 brick house with hipped roof, unfortunately much altered.

Shavington House, Cheshire. Stately brick house, 1685, 17 bays wide and 2 storeys high with attics over end 3 bays and middle 5. W side red brick with blue chequer, 9 bays with far projecting wings. Alterations in 1822, 1885 by R. N. Shaw and 1903 by E. Newton. Good staircase.

68 The Close, Salisbury, Wiltshire, 1718. A very grand detached house influenced by smaller baroque country houses

Shenstone Park, Staffordshire. Possibly by F. or W. Smith, c. 1710/20.

Shepperton Rectory, Surrey. Honington-type brick house, c. 1700.

Sherborne, Dorset. *Lord Digby's School,* Benjamin Bastard, c. 1720, simple 7-bay stone house with 3-bay centre projection, under pediment. Good staircase with wall-paintings by Thornhill.

Sherborne, Gloucestershire. *Sherborne House,* earlier house rebuilt by Valentine Strong for Col. John Dutton, 1651–3. *Lodge Park,* after 1640, for Col. Dutton. Very papery Classicism, by improbable tradition attributed to John Webb. Originally built as grandstand from which to watch deer coursing.

Shipley, West Sussex. *Newbuildings Place,* 1683, stone house with brick quoins, gabled.

Shotover Park, Oxfordshire. Begun c. 1714 for James Tyrell, perhaps by William Townesend. Plain 7-bay house with open arcaded loggia on garden side.

Shrewsbury, Shropshire. *Judge's Lodgings,* c. 1701, red brick, 6 bays and 3 storeys with interesting interiors. *Library* and *Museum* (originally School), 1590s–1630s, very Jacobean.

Siddington, Gloucestershire. *Roberts House,* C16 house greatly altered in late C17.

Simonburn, Northumberland. *Rectory,* 1725, 5 bays and 3 storeys, quoins and segment-headed windows with Gibbs surrounds. Heaviness in handling of details would indicate Vanbrughian influence rather than involvement.

Skelbrooke, South Yorkshire. *Robin Hood's Well,* Sir John Vanbrugh for Earl of Carlisle, c. 1710.

Slyfield Manor, Surrey. Early artisan mannerism, c. 1630, including S wing with giant pilasters but no entablature, directly abutting roof. Is the roof original? Wide end bay with Dutch gable.

Slyne Manor, Lancashire. Symmetrical 5-bay house, 1681, with transomed and mullioned windows.

Smedmore House, Dorset. W front of early C18 added to earlier house. Brick with stone dressings.

Snowshill, Gloucestershire. House, c. 1500, with additions C17 and C18, including wing 1700, now entrance front, with mixture of mullioned and transomed windows and sashes. (National Trust.)

Somersby Hall, Lincolnshire. Small Vanbrughian country house, 1722, perhaps to plans by Robert Alfray.

South Luffenham Hall, Leicestershire. 5-bay, 2-storey house with hipped roof and dormers of late C17.

South Malling, East Sussex. *The Deanery,* red brick late C17 house with giant pilasters and quoins. *Malling House,* 1710, grey brick with red dressings, 9 bays and 2 storeys.

Southrop, Gloucestershire. *Fyfield House,* early C18, with gabled central projection. *The Pines,* remains of early C18 house.

Southwell, Nottinghamshire. *Cranfield House,* Church St, c. 1700–20, probably for Canon George Mompesson. Brick with stone dressings, 2 storeys, hipped roof with dormers.

Spettisbury, Dorset. *Rectory,* 1716, possibly by Thomas Bastard.

Stalham Hall, Norfolk. 5-bay, 2-storey house, c. 1670, with gabled ends, 2 orders of paired brick pilasters and windows with tripartite lights and arched centres.

Stamford, Lincolnshire. *19 St George's Square,* mid-C17, gabled. *3 St Mary's Place,* early C18 Vanbrughian town house. *44 St Mary's Street,* 1656, gabled with mullioned windows.

Stanford Hall, Leicestershire. Built by William Smith the Elder for Sir Francis Cave, 1697–1700. 9 by 7 bays with S front ashlar-faced, the rest brick, hipped roof. (Open to the public.)

Stanway, Gloucestershire. *Gatehouse to Stanway House,* c. 1630, Jacobean 3-storey building with gables, shallow bay-windows on all 3 floors and central arch flanked by pair of Doric columns carrying large segmental pediment broken by pedimented frame.

Stanwell, Surrey. *Lord Knyvett's School* (104), 1624.

Stapleford Park, Leicestershire. Additions c. 1670–80, 2 storeys with quoins. S façade was Jacobeanised by Micklethwaite, 1898. Dining room with excellent wood-carving. (Open to the public.)

Staunton Harold, Leicestershire. *Church* (75), 1653–63, possibly by master mason Richard Shepherd, for Sir Robert Shirley.

Stifford, Essex. *Ford Place,* 1665, garden front with Dutch gable, entrance front late C17, yellow brick with red dressings, 9 bays and 2 storeys.

Stirling, Central Region. *Argyll's Lodging,* c. 1632, courtyard house, with turrets, but regular fenestration and much Netherlandish decoration over windows. *38 Broad St (185)*, 4-storey house with crow-stepped gable and 3 tiers of pedimented windows, dated 1671. *Cowane's Hospital,* 1635, regular E-plan with tower over door and crow-stepped gables. *Town House (115)*, Sir William Bruce, 1703–5.

Stockport, Greater Manchester. *2 Vale Road, Heaton Mersey,* mid-C17 timber house.

Stockton, Cleveland. *St Mary,* 1710–12, very typical early C18 church. Red brick, nave of 6 bays with arched windows. Tower early C19, additions by W. D. Caroë, 1925.

Stockton, Wiltshire. *Topp Almshouses,* c. 1657. Small, stone, 3-winged, 1 storey, with dormers.

Stoke Bruerne, Northamptonshire. *Stoke Park,* Inigo Jones, c. 1630, though probably not finished by him, for Sir Francis Crane. Central block demolished 1886, leaving only pavilions. (Open to the public.)

Stoke Mandeville, Buckinghamshire. *Stoke House,* c. 1700, Williamite house, 5 bays by 5 and 2 storeys, with hipped roof and good carved doorways.

Stoneleigh Abbey, Warwickshire. (47, 61.) Built for Lord Leigh by Francis Smith, 1714–26. W range 15 bays, arranged 2-3-5-3-2, with projections at middle and ends, broken by giant Ionic pilasters. Good saloon and staircase.

Stonyhurst, Lancashire. *Shireburn Almshouses,* John Mason, 1707. *Stoneyhurst House, garden pavilions,* with concave-sided roofs and 2 very thin windows either side of doorway and keystone carved as Chinaman's face. As pavilions are dated c. 1712, it is very early for chinoiserie.

Stourbridge, Hereford and Worcester. *St Thomas,* 1728–36, brick with stone dressings, nave of 4 bays with arched windows. Side galleries on Tuscan columns and panelled arched ceiling. Chancel and screen added 1890 by W H Bidlake.

Stowe, Buckinghamshire. Additions to house, perhaps including N portico and garden buildings, for Viscount Cobham by Sir John Vanbrugh, c. 1719–24.

Stratfield Saye House, Hampshire. Brick house, c. 1645, 2 storeys with 9-bay centre and 2 bay gabled wings. Altered c. 1775, 1838 by Benjamin Dean Wyatt and 1964. Little remaining of interior. (Open to the public.)

Stratford-upon-Avon, Warwickshire. *Vicarage,* now Headmaster's House, by Francis Smith, 1702–3.

Stretton-under-Fosse, Warwickshire. *Newbold Revel* (now St Paul's College), Smith type house (1716) for Sir Fulwar Skipwith, of brick with stone dressings. Altered by Edgar Wood, c. 1900.

Stroud, Gloucestershire. *Lodgemoor Mills,* Caincross, *Offices* (formerly mill-owners house), early C18 with slightly later wing.

Sudbury Hall, Derbyshire. (15, *16*, 17, 32, 33.) Built for George Vernon during 1660s and 1670s. Entrance porch sculpture carved by Sir William Wilson. Interior carving and joinery by Grinling Gibbons and Edward Pearce, and plasterwork by Robert Bradbury and James Pettifer. (National Trust.)

Sudeley, Gloucestershire. *Wadfield,* c. 1700, with hipped roof and dormers. Good contemporary interiors.

Sunderland, Tyne and Wear. *Holy Trinity,* 1719, red brick with stone dressings and arched windows. Front emphasised by giant Tuscan pilasters. Inside, flat roof supported by giant Corinthian columns.

Sutton Scarsdale, Derbyshire. (47, *47,* 61.) Built by Francis Smith for Earl of Scarsdale, begun 1724. Now ruin in care of DoE.

Sutton-upon-Tern, Shropshire. *Buntingsdale Hall,* Francis Smith for Bulkeley Mackworth, completed 1721; enlarged 1857. Brick with stone dressings with basement, 2 storeys and attic above cornice. Complex use of giant pilasters and roof-line. Some good interiors.

Swaffham Bulbeck, Cambridgeshire. *Merchant House,* c. 1700 (?), gabled brick house.

Swallowfield House, Berkshire. By William Talman, 1689–91, for Earl of Clarendon. Altered 1720–2 by John James; remodelled by W. Atkinson, 1820.

Swanage, Dorset. *Town Hall (115)*, built 1872 with addition (1883) of façade from Mercer's Hall in City of London by Edward Jarman, 1670, carved by John Young.

Swindon, Gloucestershire. *Church Cottage,* c. 1700, timber cottage.

Swinfen Hall, Staffordshire. (61.) For

Samuel Swynfen, 1755, by Benjamin Wyatt, and now part of prison. Smith type house of 2 storeys with ½ storey attic above cornice, with top balustrade and giant Ionic angle pilasters.

Swinstead, Lincolnshire. *Belvedere (116, 117)* for Duke of Ancaster by Sir John Vanbrugh (?), c. 1720.

Swynnerton Hall, Staffordshire. (61.) Built for Thomas Fitzherbert, 1725–9, possibly by Francis Smith. Altered by James Trubshawe, 1811–12, and again 1949–50 and 1974. 9 bays and 2 storeys with attic above cornice; 3-bay centre with giant Tuscan pilasters.

Sychtyn Hall, Clwyd. House, c. 1720, thoroughly Victorianised 1868.

Tadworth Court, Surrey. Yellow brick house, c. 1700, with pedimented central

36 and 38 Broad Street, Stirling, Central Region, late seventeenth century. Over-restored but otherwise fairly typical examples of early symmetrical Scottish town-house façades

projection, hipped roof and dormers. Interesting interiors including staircase.

Tamworth, Staffordshire. *Town Hall,* Market Street, 1701, stone and brick with Tuscan arcade below.

Teddington, Hereford and Worcester. *Teddington Hands,* wonderful early signpost, erected in 1676.

Temple Balsall House, West Midlands. Rebuilt by Francis Smith, 1738–9.

Tenby, Dyfed. *St Mary,* tomb of William Risam, c. 1633, and pulpit, 1634.

Tenterden, Kent. *Westwell,* 1711, 7 bays by 4 in brick with stone dressings, 2 storeys with parapet.

Tetbury, Gloucestershire. *Crown Inn,* Gumstool Hill, 1693, with blocked oval windows in gables. *Delburn House,* Gumstool Hill, early C18, 2 storeys with attic and modillion cornice. *Market House,* 1655, on Tuscan columns, altered 1817. *Porch House,* Long St, C17, gabled.

Theale, Somerset. *Great House,* 1670, 5-bay, 2-storey block with staircase of Eltham Lodge type; open-work panels depicting snake-bodied beasts, however, rather than acanthus foliage, as was usual, or military trophies, as was used at Ham House.

Theobalds Park, Hertfordshire. *Temple Bar,* 1671.

Thorganby, North Yorkshire. *St Helen,* 1690, brick church with older W tower, Classical except Perpendicular E window.

Thorney Abbey House, Cambridgeshire. Additions, perhaps by Peter Mills, to C16 house, 1660, very like Thorpe Hall. Good dining-room and staircase.

Thornton-le-Street, North Yorkshire. *Brawith Hall,* early C18, pilastered red brick house with stone dressings and high parapet. Good staircase.

Thorpe Hall, Cambridgeshire. (17, 30.) Built for Oliver St John, 1654–6, by Peter Mills. 3 storeys with string-course above ground floor, hipped roof and dormers. E side with odd fenestration and bay rhythm. Very fine interiors and staircase.

Thurstaston Hall, Merseyside. Central block, c. 1680, 3-bay and 2-storey brick front with stone dressings.

Tibberton, Hereford and Worcester. *Rectory Farmhouse,* C17, timber-framed house of 2 storeys with attic.

Tilbury, Essex. *Fort, Gate,* 1682, 2 storeys with superimposed orders and carved military trophies.

Tiverton, Devon. *St George,* John James, 1714–33. Re-roofed 1841–2.

Tong Hall, West Yorkshire. 1700–2, possibly by Theophilus Shelton for Sir George Tempest.

Tredegar Park, Gwent. (*30.*) Brick house, 1664–1674, with stone dressings.

Treyford Manor House, West Sussex. 5-bay, 2-storey house, c. 1690–1710, of clunch with brick dressings.

Trumpington, Cambridgeshire. *Anstey Hall,* c. 1700, incorporating C16 house. Interesting brick entrance front with 1-bay central projection with overlong giant Ionic columns and strange baroque pediment.

Tulliallan, Fife Region. *Church,* 1675, Classical in form but with traceried windows.

Tunbridge Wells, Kent. *King Charles the Martyr,* originally 1676–8, extended 1682 and 1688–90. Red and blue brick chequer with arched windows, original part of interior with low domes. N and W additions with octagonal domes. Good plasterwork.

Tushingham, Cheshire. *Church,* 1689–91, Gothic survival.

Twycross House, Leicestershire. Late C17 house, 5 bays by 4 with quoins and hipped roof.

Tyberton, Hereford and Worcester. *Church,* 1720, brick with semi-domed apse.

Tyttenhanger House, Hertfordshire. Perhaps by Peter Mills, 1654.

Uley, Gloucestershire. *Bencombe,* C17 gabled house. *King's Head* Inn, early C18, 2 storeys and hipped roof with dormers.

Umberslade Hall, Warwickshire. Francis Smith for Andrew Archer, c. 1695–1700, altered C19.

Uppark, West Sussex. (*10.*) William Talman for Lord Grey, c. 1690. Altered later, especially interior, including 1805 by Humphrey Repton. (National Trust.)

Upper Slaughter, Gloucestershire. *Home Farmhouse,* c. 1700, with hipped roof and dormers. *The Manor,* 1680, again with dormers.

Upton House, Warwickshire. N front, 1695, 9 bays with recessed 3-bay centre. S side also 1695, but simpler. Altered inside and out by P. Morley Horder, 1927–8. (National Trust.)

Upton Lovell, Wiltshire. *Church,* with tower and nave windows of 1633.

Ven House, Somerset. (*61.*) Built for

James Medlycott by Nathaniel Ireson, c. 1725. Later enlarged and rebuilt.

The Vyne, Hampshire. (*28.*) Alterations to interior and garden front by John Webb for Chaloner Chute, 1654–6. He may also have built the *garden house.* (National Trust.)

Wakefield, West Yorkshire. *Heath Hall Water Tower,* built mid-C17 by Lady Mary Bolles to supply water to Hall. *Kettlethorpe Hall,* c. 1727, small 5-bay block with 1-storey wings, using rather Central European pediment-types.

Waldershare Park, Kent. Plain house, c. 1705–12, with 9-bay front with pilaster-strips delineating end bays and giant Corinthian columns the centre. Rebuilt and remodelled by Sir Reginald Blomfield after 1913 fire.

Walford-on-Wye, Hereford and Worcester. *Hill Court,* 1698–1700, 7 bays, 2 storeys; attic added when enlarged (1732).

Walston, Strathclyde Region. *Church,* 1656, Gothic.

Warminster, Wiltshire. *Meeting House,* 1704, brick with stone dressings.

Warwick, Warwickshire. *Abbotsford,* Market Place, probably by Francis Smith, 1714. *Castle,* State Rooms, remodelled 1669–78, by R & W Hurlbutt, very typical of C17 decoration. *Court House* (113), Jury St, Francis Smith, 1725–30, stone with all-over rustication, upper floor articulated by Roman Doric pilasters with a good frieze. *Market House,* Roger Hurlbutt, 1670, originally with open ground-floor arcade. *St Mary,* rebuilt after fire (1694) by Sir William Wilson with possible assistance of Wren, after 1698.

Wateringbury Place, Kent. 3 storeys with attic above cornice and angle pilasters, 1707.

Wentworth Castle, South Yorkshire. (*47, 48.*) Built for Earl of Strafford, c. 1710–20, possibly to designs prepared by German architect, Jean de Bodt. In its regularity, simplicity and confining of stress to centre and ends it conforms to rather French style introduced to Dresden during 1720s by architects such as de Bodt, as well as Longuelune and Knöffel.

Weobley, Hereford and Worcester. *School,* pre-1653, timber with gabled dormers.

West Amesbury House, Wiltshire.

Later C17 flint and stone chequer house with regular fenestration.

West Boldon Hall, Tyne and Wear. Simple but grand house of 1709, stone, 5 bays and 2 storeys.

West Farleigh Hall, Kent. Brick house, c. 1720, with giant pilasters articulating central 3 bays.

West Green House, Hampshire. 5-bay front, c. 1700–30, with top battlements.

West Malling, Kent. *Went House,* c. 1720, with segment-headed windows.

West Woodhay Manor, Hampshire. Early example of compact artisan mannerist house, 1635.

Westbrook, Wiltshire. *Nonsuch,* c. 1700, typical late Stuart house of 7 bays and 2 storeys.

Westerham, Kent. *Squerries Court,* before 1686, 7 bays and 2 storeys, hipped roof with dormers, rubbed brick angle pilasters and cornice-pediment over 3 central bays.

Weston-sub-Edge, Gloucestershire. *Manor House,* late C17 with hipped roof.

Weston-under-Lizard, Staffordshire. *St Andrew,* 1700, remodelled in simple Classical style at instigation of Lady Wilbraham. *Weston Park,* 1671, perhaps by Lady Wilbraham, with broken segmental pediments over 2 bays at each end of S front. (Open to the public.)

Westwood Park, Hereford and Worcester. Diagonal wings added in later C17 to house of c. 1600, in completely Jacobean style in tune with earlier work.

Whitchurch, Shropshire. *St Alkmund,* 1712, to design by John Barker and built by William Smith of Warwick, very similar to churches at Burton-on-Trent and Lincoln.

Whitehaven, Cumbria. Earliest post-Reformation town-plan in England, by Sir John Lowther as coal-port during 1680s.

Wigan, Greater Manchester. *Haigh South Outfall,* 1653, one of earliest colliery drainage schemes in Lancashire coalfield, extended in C19.

Willen, Buckinghamshire. *Church* (88), Robert Hooke, 1680, lead cupola removed 1814; apse added 1862.

Williamstoun Castle, Tayside Region. Plain T-plan tower-house, c. 1650.

Wilmslow, Cheshire. *Presbyterian* (now Congregational) *Chapel,* Dean Row, 1693, Jacobean vernacular survival.

Wilton House, Wiltshire. (27, *27.*) Built by Isaac de Caus for Earl of Pembroke, 1636. Gutted c. 1648 and rebuilt by Webb; subsequently modifications by Webb including towers and State Rooms in S front. *Park Schoolhouse,* 1638, incorporating grotto by de Caus with decoration by Nicholas Stone II.

Wimborne Minster, Dorset. *Dean's Court,* 1725, brick with stone dressings, top parapet and 3-bay centre projections to main façades.

Wimpole Hall, Cambridgeshire. House built in stages, c. 1640, c. 1700, and 1719–21 by James Gibbs, who added chapel and garden front. Chapel good example of illusionist decoration by Sir James Thornhill. Altered by Sir John Soane, 1791–3.

Wincanton, Somerset. *Church,* Nathaniel Ireson rebuilt chancel, added clerestory, re-roofed and re-windowed nave, 1748, all at own expense. Also built *Ireson House* for himself c. 1726, altered c. 1851; *Hillside House,* early to mid C18; rebuilt *White Horse Inn,* 1733; *Balsam House, Robber House,* alterations, c. 1730; *The Dogs,* Tout Hill, c. 1745.

Winchcombe, Gloucestershire. *Great House,* Castle St, late C17 with hipped roof. *Jacobean House,* C17 with outside staircase and gables.

Winchester, Hampshire. *Cathedral, Rood Screen,* possibly by Inigo Jones, 1637–8. Dismantled in 1820; central part now in Museum of Archaeology, Cambridge. *Bishop's House,* 1684, rather old-fashioned house with hipped roof. *College Chapel,* furnishings, 1680–3, with communion rail by Edward Pierce. *College, New Schoolroom* (104), 1683, beautiful 7-bay brick building with stone dressings and hipped roof. *Guildhall* (now Lloyd's Bank), 1713. Open Tuscan columned ground floor, now closed; above, statue of Queen Anne in niche and good clock-bracket. *Serle's House* (now Regimental Museum), c. 1710–20, very Baroque, but more that of Archer than of Vanbrugh or Hawksmoor (compare with Chettle). *Southgate Hotel,* Southgate St, 1715, 5 bays and 3 storeys with segment-headed windows.

Windsor, Berkshire. *Castle* (40, 41, *41,* 42, 43), Hugh May for King Charles II, after 1674. Remodelling of upper ward, including St George's Hall and King's Chapel, and Apartments for King and Queen. Ceilings decorated by Verrio.

Masonic Hall, 1725–6, small brick building rather Hawksmoorian in style. *Old House Hotel*, just pre-1700 with projecting, differing wings. *Town Hall*, c. 1687–90, by Sir Thomas Fitch with open ground floor with brick upper floor. *Park, Pump House*, 1718, probably by Sir John Vanbrugh.

Winkburn Hall, Nottinghamshire. Brick house of 1700 with attic above cornice and slight central recesses on main fronts.

Winslow Hall, Buckinghamshire. Sir Christopher Wren (?) for William Lowndes, 1699–1702. Tall brick house with hipped roof and tall chimneys.

Winson, Gloucestershire. *Manor Farm*, late C17 house with hipped roof and dormers.

Wintoun House, Lothian Region. Well-decorated L-shaped house, probably built by William Wallace, 1620, with orders and decoration around windows. Tall spiral ornamented chimneys, cornice and parapet of square tower suggest English influence.

Wisbech, Cambridgeshire. *Castle*, possibly by Peter Mills, 1655–7. *Peckover House*, North Brink, shortly before 1727, yellow brick with red dressings with segment-headed windows. Good later C18 interiors. (National Trust.)

Withcote Hall, Leicestershire. Early C18 house, 7 bays and 2 storeys with a 3-bay pediment on entrance-front and projecting wings towards garden.

Withington, Gloucestershire. *Foxcote Manor*, late C17 with hipped roof.

Witney, Oxfordshire. *Grammar School* (104), Church Green, 1660. Typical early post-Restoration school.

Wokingham, Berkshire. *Lucas Hospital* (99), 1665, brick in Restoration style, long and low with wings and 3-bay pediment in centre, cupola above.

Wolverton, Hampshire. *St Catherine*, 1717, large W tower of brick with stone quoins, main church of red brick with blue dressings. This was the recasing of older church.

Woodbury, Devon. *Brown's Farmhouse*, c. 1700, cob.

Woodstock, Oxfordshire. *Hope House* (70), Hensington Rd, c. 1720, with side wall of blind, arched, flat niches. Bow windows to front of house added later. *Rectory*, Rectory Lane, C17, remodelled early C18, with towers flanking typical original gable. Garden front very strange

with definite Hawksmoor-Vanbrugh look.

Woolmet House, Lothian Region. Irregularly planned house of 1686, but with regular fenestration.

Wootton Bassett, Wiltshire. *Town Hall*, given by Earl of Rochester, 1700, with open ground floor and timberframed upper floor.

Wootton Wawen, Warwickshire. *Wootton Hall*, 1687, 9 bays by 9, slightly projecting pedimented 3-bay centre.

Worcester, Hereford and Worcester. *All Saints*, attributed to Thomas White, 1738–42, with 6-bay, aisled nave and segmental chancel vault. Façade with giant triangular pediment supported by doubled Doric pilasters framing large, round-headed windows. *St Nicholas*, attributed to Thomas White, 1730–5, façade with giant Doric pilasters and central giant segmental pediment on cornice. 4-bay nave with arched windows. *St Swithun*, Thomas and Edward Woodward. 1734–6, with central Venetian window on façade framed by pair of Doric pilasters topped by large triangular pediment. *Britannia House*, Upper Tything (now Headmistress's House of Alice Ottley School), c. 1725, with centre emphasised by elaboration of door-surround and that of 1st floor window. *Town Hall* (113, *115*), probably by Thomas White, 1721–4, designs apparently handed in in 1718.

Worfield, Shropshire. *Davenport House*, Smith type house, 1726, in brick with stone dressings, with hipped roof over attic, parapet and heavy 2nd-storey cornice.

Worsborough, South Yorkshire. *Rockley Furnace and Engine House*, 1652, one of most important examples of early blast furnaces, later reworked c. 1800.

Wotton House, Buckinghamshire. (62.) Brick house, c. 1704, with stone dressings and angle pilasters, 2 delightful 1-storey pavilions. Much altered later. (Open to the public.)

Wrest Park, Bedfordshire. *Garden Pavilion*, Thomas Archer, 1709–11, domed on triangular plan, probably influenced by pavilion by Fischer von Erlach at Schloss Klesheim near Salzburg.

Wymondham, Norfolk. *Cavick House*, typical early C18 house in brick with hipped roof.

Wynnstay House, Clwyd. Francis and

William Smith II, 1736–9.

Yarm, Cleveland. *Kelton Ox* (70), High St, odd house, c. 1670, with 3 tiers of pilasters, originally in brick; oval windows in attic originally open. *Town Hall*, High St, 1710, brick, of 2 bays, with hipped roof and lantern; ground floor later closed.

Yazor, Hereford and Worcester. *House*, c. 1700, timber on stone plinth.

Yester House, Lothian Region. James Smith and Alexander McGill, possibly with advice from Bruce, 1700–15. House undecorated, except for horizontal rustication and attached Ionic portico supporting cornice and pediments like those over end pavilions of colonnades at Greenwich. Garden side completely plain but with similar pediment motif above cornice. Altered by William Adam, 1730, and by Robert Adam, 1788.

York, North Yorkshire. *Cromwell House*, Ogleforth, c. 1700, 5 bays and 2 storeys with large gable towards street. *Cumberland's House*, King's Staith, c. 1695, brick with stone quoins. *Judge's Lodging*, Lendal, 1718–25, brick with giant pilasters. Beautiful entrance hall.

BIBLIOGRAPHY

Place of publication is London unless
otherwise stated.

Airs, M., *The Making of the English Country House, 1500–1640*, 1975.

Beard, G., *Decorative Plasterwork in Great Britain*, 1975.

Beazley, E., and Howell, P., *The Companion Guide to North Wales*, 1975.
The Companion Guide to South Wales, 1977.

Blunt, A., ed., *Baroque and Rococo, Architecture and Decoration*, 1978.

Downes, K., *English Baroque Architecture*, 1966.
Vanbrugh, 1977.
Hawksmoor, 1979.
Sir Christopher Wren, 1982.

Dunbar, J. G., *The Historic Architecture of Scotland*, 1966.
Sir William Bruce, exhibition catalogue, Scottish Arts Council, 1970.

Fleming, J., *Robert Adam and his Circle*, 1962.

Girouard, M., *Life in the English Country House*, New Haven and London, 1978.

Godfrey, W. H., *The English Almshouse*, 1955.

Harris, J., *The Palladians*, 1981.

Hay, G., *The Architecture of Scottish Post-Reformation Churches, 1560–1843*, Oxford, 1957.

Hilling, J. B., *The Historical Architecture of Wales*, Cardiff, 1976.

Mercer, E., *English Vernacular Houses*, 1975.

Pevsner, N., *The Buildings of England*, Harmondsworth, 1951–74.

Seaborne, M., *The English School*, esp. Vol. 1, 1971.

Smith, P., *Houses of the Welsh Countryside*, 1975.

Summerson, Sir J., *Architecture in Britain 1530 to 1830*, Harmondsworth, 1953, 4th ed. 1963.
Inigo Jones, Harmondsworth, 1966.
The Classical Language of Architecture, 1980.

Whiffen, M., *Stuart and Georgian Churches*, 1947/48.

Whistler, L., *The Imagination of Sir John Vanbrugh and his Fellow Artists*, 1954.

INDEX OF ARCHITECTS, MASONS AND BUILDERS

ILLUSTRATION ACKNOWLEDGEMENTS

Photographs are reproduced on the pages specified
by kind permission of the following:

The British Library (14, 20, 58 *below*); the British
Museum (12); *Country Life* – photos by Alex Starkey
(36, 37, 38, 39); Courtauld Institute of Art (83);
Kerry Downes (33, 44, 54, 56, 61, 82 *above*, 85, 91
both, 93 *both*, 94, 102 *both*, 105, 110 *both*, 111, 114
both, 115, 118 *below*, 145, 147, 163, 167, 174, 178);
Guildhall Library (76 *below*); A. F. Kersting (26, 34,
49 *above*, 65, 72, 78, 90, 109, 155, 179); Richard
Morrice (24, 109 *both*, 169 *below*); Peter Spokes
(108).

Reproduced by gracious permission of Her Majesty
The Queen (38 *above*, 41).

Crown Copyright – reproduced by permission of the
Controller of the Copyright Section, Publications
Division, Her Majesty's Stationery Office; National
Monuments Record (10, 15, 16, 25 *both*, 27, 29, 31,

32, 42, 43, 46, 47, 48, 49 *below*, 51, 53, 58 *above*, 60
both, 62, 63, 64, 67, 69 *above*, 71, 73 *both*, 74, 76 *above*,
77, 80, 81, 82 *below*, 86, 87 *both*, 88, 92, 96 *both*, 97,
101, 103, 104, 112, 116 *both*, 117, 118 *above*, 149,
152, 161, 162, 165, 169 *above*, 175, 177, 182); the
Scottish Development Department (98, 185); the
Royal Commission on Ancient and Historical
Monuments in Wales (30, 69 *below*, 140, 180).

Plans are reproduced on the pages specified, by
permission, from the following sources:

Kerry Downes, *English Baroque Architecture*, A.
Zwemmer, 1966 (41, 52, 92); Kerry Downes, *Sir
Christopher Wren*, Allen Lane, 1971 (79, 81, 83, 84,
100 – 1); Mark Girouard, *Life in the English Country
House*, Yale University Press, 1978 (29, 45); W. H.
Godfrey, *The English Almshouse*, Batsford, 1955
(100); Sir John Summerson, *Architecture in Britain
1530 – 1830*, Pelican, 1963 (26, 35).